PATTERNITY

A NEW WAY OF SEEING

The Inspirational Power of Pattern

Anna Murray & Grace Winteringham

Contributing Editor Dal Chodha

conran
OCTOPUS

An Hachette UK Company
www.hachette.co.uk

First published in Great Britain in 2015 by Conran
Octopus, a division of Octopus Publishing Group Ltd
Carmelite House, 50 Victoria Embankment,
London EC4Y 0DZ
www.octopusbooks.co.uk
www.octopusbooksusa.com

Design and layout copyright © PATTERNITY Limited 2015
Text copyright © PATTERNITY Limited 2015

Distributed in the US by Hachette Book Group
1290 Avenue of the Americas, 4th and 5th Floors,
New York, NY 10020

Distributed in Canada by Canadian Manda Group
664 Annette St., Toronto, Ontario, Canada M6S 2C8

ISBN 978 1 84091 694 2

A CIP catalogue record for this book is available from the
British Library.

Printed and bound in China

10 9 8 7 6 5 4 3 2 1

Commissioning Editor: Joe Cottington
Editor: Pollyanna Poulter
Copy Editor: Jane Ace
Proofreader: Zia Mattocks
Indexer: Vanessa Bird
Art Director: Juliette Norsworthy
Creative Direction & Design: PATTERNITY
Researcher: Didi Wambugu
Picture Editor: Liv Taylor
Production Controller: Sarah Kramer

'Because a shared awareness and understanding of pattern will positively shape the future.'

PATTERNITY

Page 4, Vent Lines, PATTERNITY, Sydney | Page 5, Mono Man, Mark Pillai, Kriss Van Assche for Dior Homme | Page 6, Palm Streamers, Goa, India | Page 7, Gold Drapes, Kevin Francis Gray, bronze, automotive paint, wood | Page 8, Technicolour Weave, Bernard Frize, acrylic and resin on canvas | Page 9, Trellis Trousers, Nik Hartley, jacket: Acne Studios, rollneck: Uniqlo, trousers: Issey Miyake | Page 10 Mountain Pleats, PATTERNITY, Himalayas | Page 11, Creased Collection, Nicolas Coulomb, Études

'Greatness' exists in the inconspicuous and overlooked details.'

Leonard Koren (1948–), American poet

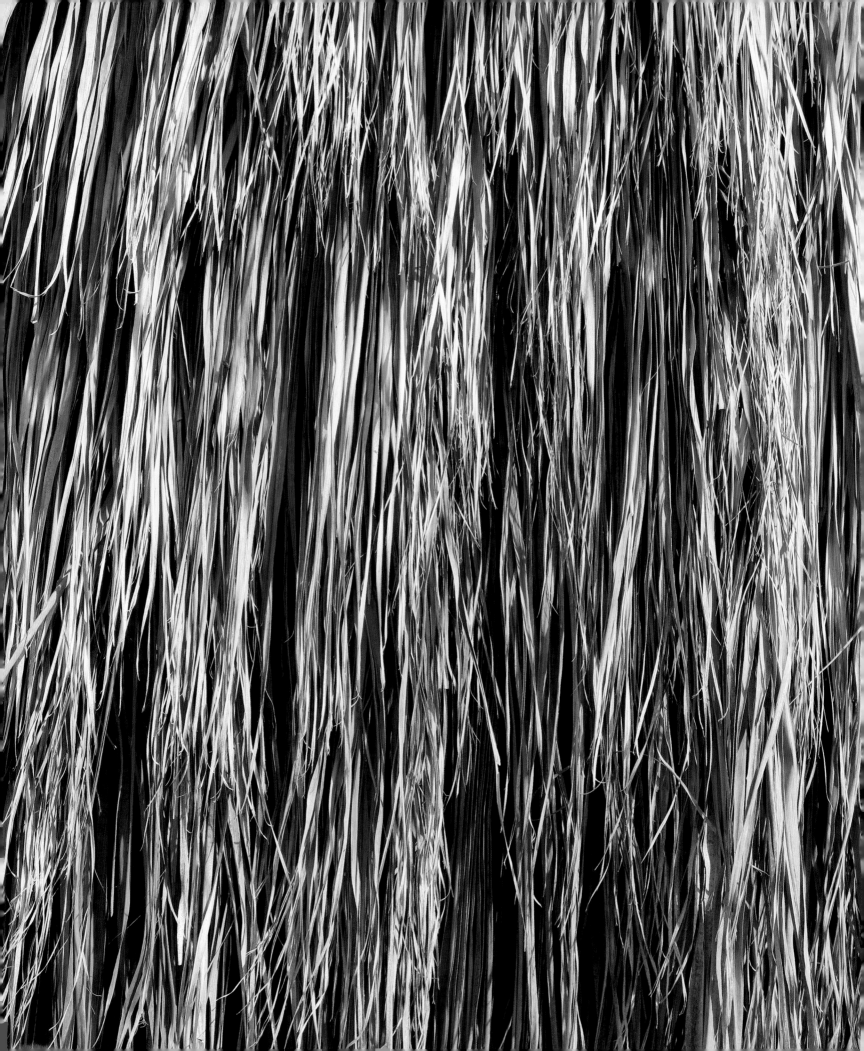

PROJECT KEY

∞   COLLABORATION

●●   EVENT

◆   SPECIAL PROJECT

▶   FILM/ANIMATION

■   PRODUCT

CONTENTS

FOREWORDS 14

PATTERN IS LIFE | AN INTRODUCTION
18
A NEW WAY OF SEEING

PART ONE | CURIOSITY
22
PATTERN INSPIRATION
Inspiring awareness and curiosity – from the
shadows below, to the clouds high above.

PART TWO | COLLABORATION
100
PATTERN INNOVATION
Championing cross-disciplinary collaboration –
from marbles to microscopic molecules.

PART THREE | CONNECTIVITY
142
PATTERN EXPLORATION
Exploring interconnectivity and scale –
from a spiralling seashell to the eye of a storm.

PATTERN IS LIFE | A CONTINUATION
202
A NEW WAY OF BEING

FURTHER READING 214
JOIN US 216
IMAGE CREDITS 217
INDEX 220
WITH GRATITUDE 223
ABOUT PATTERNITY 224

HOLLY FULTON

PHILIP BALL

I grew up engulfed in pattern and colour; my mother cannot walk down the street without marvelling at drain covers. A multitude of tiny, Fritz Lang-inspired faces stare back at her, informing her vision of the world, doubtless making it a much more stimulating place to be.

Naturally, I used clothing as the canvas to convey this graphic tutelage. In a world in danger of streamlining the foibles and quirks in its routine into oblivion, harnessing your mood and personality through your choice of pattern is a fundamental tool. For me it is as simple as this: pattern makes me happy. It has the power to elevate me as a person and alter both my mood and feelings. Pattern makes me feel strong. It adds a veneer of confidence to my everyday, and the ritual of selection provides endless inspiration.

Nothing exhilarates one more than seeing a colourful character. It can bring feelings of disbelief, respect, joy. This is the power of pattern on both the wearer and the observer; it shapes the social landscape and contributes to the stratum of society, whether through the following of trends, the ritualistic traditions of culture or the simple desire to break free from the norm.

PATTERNITY harness the unexpected and make us reassess our surroundings and our vision of the world, allowing us to elevate the mundane and revel in the chaos and clarity pattern can provide. They excite us and enable us to fuel both our imagination and our environment.

We live our life through patterns. Our brains are attuned to finding regularities in the world and using them to make predictions and deductions. That ability is the source of all science, of language and culture, of our sense of place in the cosmos. Repetition and organization of form lies at the root of our arts and crafts: we build this way, make music this way, and create new technologies and social structures. No wonder, then, that our brains aren't just adept at finding order and pattern, but respond to it aesthetically, rewarding ourselves with the pleasure and satisfaction of seeing universal harmonies.

It is the intrinsic tendency of the natural world to produce pattern and form that has allowed life to appear and evolve. In one view, this is not some astonishing coincidence peculiar to our lucky circumstance but is an almost inevitable consequence of the basic laws of nature. By delving into questions of how pattern arises, we might therefore address some of the most fundamental questions about the world.

And we learn handy tricks: how to rely on spontaneous self-organization, rather than laborious piece-by-piece placement, to achieve orderly structures that might be useful to us, whether those are the arrays of microscopic components in computer circuits or the spatial arrangements of our cities. For all these reasons, a project like this book, which raises awareness of the patterns that surround us and the deep connections and analogies between them, serves a valuable purpose. These images unite the designed with the spontaneous, the beautiful with the practical and the natural with the artificial. Enjoy them.

Holly Fulton is a Scottish-born womenswear and
accessories designer living and working in East London.
A graduate from the Royal College of Art, she established
her eponymous label in 2009 after working in London and
Paris. She has developed her own unique visual language,
much loved by pattern spotters around the globe.

Philip Ball is a freelance writer, who worked previously
for more than 20 years as an editor for *Nature*. Philip
trained as a chemist at the University of Oxford and
as a physicist at the University of Bristol. He writes
regularly for the scientific and popular media, and has
authored many books on the interactions of the sciences,
the arts and the wider culture. His latest book is
Invisible: The Dangerous Allure of the Unseen (2014).

TOM DIXON

ROBERT ROWLAND SMITH

The building blocks that were my first ever toys, the holes in Meccano that then became the gears, cogs and chains on my bicycle that I would take apart and then rebuild: it is only later on that I have begun to sense the underlying patterns in everything that surrounds us. The strings of a guitar crossing the frets on the neck forming a grid of squares bringing with it so much potential for sound influenced me when I first started putting objects together.

Were you a scientist you might delve deeper into the cells of a plant or the structures of molecules but as a designer, we are instinctively stepping into and out of underlying geometries and patterns in order to reshape our world, from the invisible XYZ axes and binary codes on graph paper to the grain of wood and houndstooth cloth.

So, when PATTERNITY come with total enthusiasm, wonderment and expertise, re-presenting the omnipresent that we become immune to, we can only be grateful to them for refreshing our eyes and beyond. They categorise, decode and re-present pattern to rekindle our imagination.

As a philosopher I have learned how to look for order in arguments, theories and propositions. Typically, philosophical order takes the form of 'reason', but it's interesting that the Latin word for reason is *ratio*, which is where we get the English word 'ratio', as in 'proportion'. In other words, reason is not about logic per se, but mental harmony, order and pattern. Where those things break down, we have the opposite of reason – irrationality, disorder and disruption. In this sense, pattern is the very principle of reason.

In my own work, I am specifically looking for order and pattern in the systems in which we all belong. One of the key patterns I look for is whether people stand well in the flow of time, that they are not out of sync with where they should be.

It's important that we respect those who came before us, and that we see ourselves as following on from them, rather than blocking them out. It's this that allows us to get in tune with the force of time and allow it to pass through us onto those who come later. Although we have a notion of geniuses as people who were 'out of time', it's generally better if we belong to time's onward pattern, as it allows creativity to flow through us the better.

PATTERNITY: A New Way Of Seeing takes us both above and below the line of pattern, into both the visible and the invisible. What it reveals is that pattern is neither just an accident of nature nor solely the result of human labour, but a structuring force that appears to tie together, either consciously or unconsciously, nearly all of the phenomena we encounter.

```
Tom Dixon is a self-taught British designer famed
for his 'vertebrate' approach to design. Tackling
each project from the bones outwards, his interest
in substance over surface led to him being awarded
an OBE for services to British Design in 2001.
Creative director of UK furniture retailer Habitat
from 1998-2008, Tom is now creative director of
his own namesake brand specializing in lighting,
furniture and accessories. His work sits in museum
collections across the globe, including London's
Victoria and Albert Museum, New York's Museum of
Modern Art and Paris' Centre Pompidou.
```

```
Robert Rowland Smith is a writer and lecturer on philosophy,
literature and psychoanalysis. A founding faculty member
of The School of Life, Robert's 'New Constellations'
interactive events look at how a greater awareness and
understanding of our personal patterns or 'constellations'
can lead to increased positivity and productivity.
```

PATTERN

(n. adj.)
'(pat(ə)n)'

Origin

Middle English *patron* 'something serving as a model'. The change in sense denotes a patron giving an example to be copied. *Patron* Middle English from Old French, from Latin *patronus* 'protector of clients, defender', from *pater*, *patr–* 'father'.

PATTERN   1. A repeated decorative design   2. An arrangement regularly found in comparable objects   3. A regular and intelligible form or sequence

-ITY

(suffix)

-ə.t̬i

Origin

Meaning 'condition or quality of being' from Middle English –*ite*, from Old French –*ité* and directly from Latin –*itatem* suffix denoting state or condition, composed of connective. A word suffixed by –*ity* usually means the quality of being what the adjective describes, a word suffixed by –*ism* describes the disposition, or collectively all those who feel it.

4. Give something a form based on that of something else

5. An example for others to follow

PATTERN IS LIFE | AN INTRODUCTION

A NEW WAY OF SEEING

'The real voyage of discovery consists not in seeking new lands but seeing with new eyes.'

Marcel Proust (1871–1922), novelist

We all encounter pattern every day: whether deep in the concrete belly of a metropolitan city or perched on a verdant hillside, the patterns in everyday life reveal themselves no matter where we are in myriad ways. We wear them and we walk over them, we eat them and drink them, we even learn, think and speak in patterns. As well as being part of the basic structure of the human body and mind, patterns speak a powerful universal language.

When we launched PATTERNITY in 2009, our aim was to establish an inclusive and long-lasting organization with a bold ambition – to use pattern to inspire others to see the world differently. PATTERNITY was conceived to celebrate the infinite and omnipresence of pattern. To use pattern to better understand life.

In an increasingly complex, materialistic and fast-paced world, flooded with large conglomerates and vast amounts of waste, we wanted to 'break the pattern'; we set out to create a company with longevity, grounded by principles and values that will (we hope) outlive us as founders. Our aim was to embark on a voyage of discovery using pattern to explore many of the complex dilemmas of our time. We wanted to use pattern as an antidote to humankind's mounting disconnection and sense of isolation; to promote a 'new way of seeing' that starts with finding magnificence in the mundane.

To recognize the beauty in the seemingly banal is to foster a new kind of awareness that extends beyond our immediate surroundings. Reminding ourselves of our place within the bigger picture can help us to put our day-to-day concerns into perspective. To observe the overlooked and consider coincidence is to find an enduring sense of connection to our environment and to each other – a connection that can begin by opening our eyes.

At the dawn of PATTERNITY, we looked first to the repetitive shapes and structures of our everyday urban surroundings for inspiration. We were drawn to bold, geometric, monochrome patterns, whether graphic stripes painted on the walls of an art gallery, the slatted grid of an iron drain cover or the serried windows of an apartment block. This recognizable aesthetic was easily accessible and allowed us to spread the PATTERNITY ethos far and wide, giving pattern in its many guises the voice and platform it richly deserves.

Over time, our pattern-focused research, creative collaborations and educational events have taken us further afield, leading us to explore the patterns that connect the man-made with nature. Venturing deeper still, our knowledge and understanding of both the visual and non-visual patterns that shape life, from the microscopic to the cosmic, have influenced our direction and defined our perspective. From art and design to music, mathematics, science, spirituality and beyond, pattern has a powerful ability to unify worlds, skills and disciplines to positive effect. This cross-pollination and inclusivity is fundamental to PATTERNITY and continues to be the defining feature of our philosophy today.

More than just seeing patterns, PATTERNITY seeks to draw inspiration from them, to learn from them and engage with them. Overloaded with the barrage of everyday life, so busy travelling from A to B, absorbed by our screens and endless notifications, we have forgotten how and where to look: everyone, no matter where they are, can benefit from rediscovering a sense of wonder.

It is impossible to journey very far into the inspirational power of pattern without beginning to ask deep-rooted questions about existence and the way we live. Our research has provided us with a diverse and unique documentation of life. Studying pattern has allowed us to dig beneath the surface and collaborate with many different disciplines and specialists, branching out from our own specialisms within art and design into many other fields. Along the way we have unearthed timely scientific, theoretical and philosophical points of view, both old and new, many of which are included in this book.

For those who seek to understand it, pattern is a highly creative force. These pages serve as not only a collation of innovative, pattern-focused projects and phenomena, but also an historical account of the world in which we experience them. Pattern, in all of the forms explored here, is vastly inspiring and its effects can be wide-reaching. This book aims to challenge the conception of what 'pattern' is, venturing beyond the surface to explore the potential uses of pattern to positively shape our collective future.

As with all of our projects, *PATTERNITY: A New Way Of Seeing* aims to use the power of pattern as a catalyst: to surprise, to rouse curiosity, and to bring disparate specialisms together and spark unexpected outcomes. The core themes explored throughout these pages delve into the questions that lie at the heart of our practice: Can challenging our perception of the everyday positively affect the world around us? Does being more mindful make us happier and healthier? How can seeing the smaller details enhance our understanding of the bigger picture? And, if we dare to visualize the unseen, can it drive forward innovation?

All of these questions, and many more besides, will be answered on our voyage of pattern discovery, as we explore a personally curated selection of the most inspiring patterns and pattern makers from the past, present and future.

We hope this book will be as much of a journey of exploration for its readers as it has been for us putting it together.

On behalf of PATTERNITY | Anna Murray + Grace Winteringham | PATTERNITY co-founders

Pages 20—21, Quarry Block Out, Georges Antoni, tights: PATTERNITY

'The true secret of happiness lies in taking a genuine interest in all the details of daily life.'

William Morris (1834—1896), textile designer, socialist and father of the Arts & Crafts Movement

PART ONE

CURIOSITY

INSPIRATION | FROM THE MUNDANE
TO THE MAGNIFICENT

Page 24, Rectangle Repeat, PATTERNITY, Rio de Janiero, Brazil | Page 25, Conscious Cloth, Sarah Piantadosi, cashmere jumper and grid jersey: PATTERNITY ∞ Chinti + Parker | Page 26, Shutter Chevrons, PATTERNITY, East London | Page 27, Line Lady, Rory DCS, jacket: vintage Versace, swimsuit: vintage

VENDO
6276.9945

'The first and simplest emotion which we discover in the human mind, is curiosity.'

Edmund Burke (1729–1797), author, political theorist and philosopher

Page 28, Cable Spray, PATTERNITY, Anzac Bridge, Sydney | Page 29, Tassel Triangle, Amy Gwatkin, fashion: Yulia Kondranina

'He who can no longer pause to wonder and stand rapt in awe, is as good as dead; his eyes are closed.'

Albert Einstein (1879–1955), German-born theoretical physicist and philosopher of science

Bubbles formed in a glass of water overnight look curiously like stars within the cosmos.

Designers, including David David, incorporate pattern into their work in infinitely inspiring ways from underwear to umbrellas and tiles to T-shirts.

THE POWER OF CURIOSITY | HEIGHTENING AWARENESS

How often do you notice the magnificent in the mundane? Have you ever stopped to see how shadows make patterns all around us on sunny days, or taken a second on your drizzly commute to marvel at the Technicolor swirls of diesel that make rainbows within puddles? Have you ever noticed how the tiny bubbles in a glass of water are reminiscent of a starry sky?

When you pause to look around, you will see that we are always surrounded by pattern. In a chaotic world overloaded with sensory stimulation, observing the fundamental formations that shape our everyday lives can provide familiarity and calm. Today's world is so cluttered and confusing that it's often difficult to know where to focus. Modern life has become so saturated with attention-grabbing imagery and we are too busy looking for the 'next best thing' to notice that the artistry in art and design has almost become irrelevant. In a world stretched for time, deluged by information and paralysed by choice, PATTERNITY believes that a quiet observation and understanding of pattern can help us to find clarity and contentment amid the overload.

Today a host of artists and designers, such as Yayoi Kusama, Tauba Auerbach, Issey Miyake and Gareth Pugh, are exploring the endless variations of pattern in their canvases and catwalk collections. Historically, however, the study of pattern was more prevalent in philosophy and the sciences, and many renowned figures dedicated their careers to understanding life through the examination of shapes and patterns.

> *'To understand is to perceive patterns.'*
> *Isaiah Berlin (1909–1997), philosopher*
> *and social and political theorist*

PATTERN THROUGH TIME | A FORGOTTEN FOCUS

The study of pattern and geometric formations links many of the most highly respected and innovative thinkers in human history. Dedicated research into pattern and the implementation of it has long acted as a gateway to making sense of the world and our place within it. As early as the 6th century BC, the Pythagoreans of ancient Greece looked to geometry to help them find answers to universal questions. So firm was the Greek's focus on this branch of mathematics and its associated shapes and patterns, that Plato's academy in Athens was said to have had a sign above its entrance that read: 'Let no one unacquainted with geometry enter here.'

A millennium later the Italian astronomer and philosopher Galileo Galilei (1564–1642), a key figure in the scientific and cultural revolution of the Renaissance, also sought answers to the fundamental problems of existence through the patterns of geometry, writing in *The Assayer (Il Saggiatore)* (1623): 'Philosophy is written in this grand book, the universe, which stands continually open to our gaze. But the book

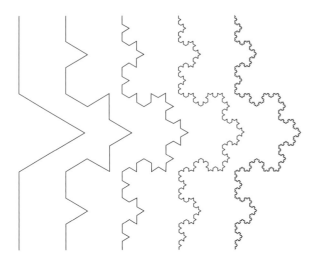

The complex fractal structure of the Koch snowflake is revealed by the application of simple mathematical rules.

cannot be understood unless one first learns to comprehend the language and to read the letters in which it is composed. It is written in the language of mathematics, and its characters are triangles, circles, and other geometric figures, without which it is humanly impossible to understand a single word of it; without these, one goes wandering about in a dark labyrinth.'

Galileo's explorations influenced countless Renaissance thinkers as well as those of the 17th century 'age of enlightenment' (whose cold, impartial observations, in turn, inspired the awe and wonderment of the Romantic poets of the 18th century). The English naturalist Charles Darwin (1809–1882) made a systematic study of the regularities and irregularities of the natural world, leading to his ground-breaking theory of evolution, *On the Origin of Species* (1859), in which he illustrated the links between species using methodical branching patterns.

In the 20th century French mathematician Benoît Mandelbrot (1924–2010) conceived a new sort of geometry after studying what he described as 'fractal' pattern formations in the natural world. In *The Fractal Geometry of Nature* (1982) he writes: 'Most of nature is very, very complicated. How could one describe a cloud? A cloud is not a sphere … It is like a ball but very irregular. A mountain? A mountain is not a cone … If you want to speak of clouds, of mountains, of rivers, of lightning, the geometric language of school is inadequate.'

Mandelbrot examined the geometry of a wide variety of irregular natural phenomena, from clouds to cauliflowers, and he realized that all of these forms had some strikingly common features. There was a pattern to be found in certain aspects of nature that could not be described in established mathematical terms.

At the same time Mandelbrot was developing his 'language to speak of clouds' in order to describe and analyse the complexity of the irregular patterns in the natural world, English anthropologist and social scientist Gregory Bateson (1904–1980) proposed that humans are instinctively pattern-seeking creatures. He wrote in *Mind and Nature: A Necessary Unity* (1979): 'Do you ask, "What is it made of – earth, fire, water, etc.?" Or do you ask, "What is its pattern?" What is the pattern that connects the crab to the lobster and the orchid to the primrose, and all four of them to me? And me to you?'. There is as much value in questioning the more fundamental 'why' as there is in seeking to answer the 'what'. Bateson, who used his pattern curiosity to traverse fields and disciplines, thought that in order to describe our everyday surroundings accurately one should try to speak nature's language, which, he insisted, is a language of relationships: the universal language of pattern.

Viewed far away or up-close, a cloud and a cauliflower speak the same universal language.

'*What is a story that it may connect the As and the Bs, its parts? And is it true that the general fact that parts are connected in this way is at the very root of what it is to be alive? I offer you the notion of context of pattern through time.*'
Gregory Bateson (1904–80), anthropologist
and social scientist

31

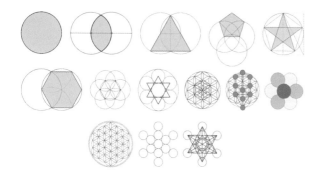

The principal elements of sacred geometry, these are the simple shapes that construct our universe.

Pattern reveals itself in the bold textures seen at London Fashion Week.

A PATTERN RENAISSANCE | PICKING UP THE THREADS

Despite its ancient origins, the research and exploration of matter (what things are made of) has generally eclipsed the study of pattern (how things are organized), which has been the preserve of a relatively small elite of segregated specialists. However, today the investigation and understanding of what Bateson called 'the pattern that connects' is experiencing a revival, merging boundaries between previously distinct disciplines and generating new discoveries.

Pattern is once again taking its place as an essential tool for driving forward collective knowledge and greater understanding of our world. This interest is evident in many different disciplines: from mathematics to music, anthropology to art, economics to ecology, sociology to science, healthcare and beyond. American educator and mathematician Michael S Schneider (1951–), author of *A Beginner's Guide to Constructing the Universe* (2003), describes this growing regard for pattern as a 'rip tide' – a timely revival in the awareness of the fundamental formations that shape the cosmos. Schneider has dedicated much of his career to popularizing the mathematics of fundamental forms and patterns, with the aim of encouraging an increased awareness and understanding of the very simple shapes and their variations that surround us all.

At surface level this revived interest is demonstrated by an increased desire to integrate pattern into our homes and wardrobes (examples of which are represented throughout this book). Pattern is perhaps at its most primal and recognizable in the world of fashion; what begins as a niche trend is often quickly adopted by many all around the world. American artist and former member of the Forcefield art collective, Jim Drain (1975–), notes in the catalogue accompanying Turner Contemporary's 2009 pattern-focused exhibition *Superabundant*: 'Pattern often is a constructive thing, takes a position, has intention, seeks to order or allows for order.' With its roots in uniform, pattern in fashion and apparel serves as an indicator that highlights a fundamental human need and survival instinct to belong and to be accepted into a tribe.

In a similar vein, the 2008 exhibition *Exactitudes* at Selfridges, London, by Dutch photographer Ari Versluis and stylist Ellie Uyttenbroek, explored the notion of individuality through dress. The exhibition showcased groups of individuals, linked by their clothing choices, in repeated grids that drew attention to how we use colour, shape and pattern to mark our place within, or outside of, a group. With so many options as to how we represent ourselves today, pattern can help us to affirm our place in the world in this Instagram age. The bold checks of a kilt, the diamond quilting of a Chanel bag or the stripes of a sports shoe can shape our sense of belonging to a wider social sphere (or hashtag).

Turing markings on Mandarinfish bring to mind
the patterns that have shaped our evolution.

Our lives are all interwoven patterns
of interaction.

PATTERN SEEKING CREATURES | AN INNATE DRIVE

Beyond the adoption of passing trends and surface decoration, humans are, as Bateson suggests, hardwired to identify systems and sequences. Throughout history our innate drive to seek patterns has shaped our very evolution. Just as patterns are fundamental to the communication of warnings and messages within the animal kingdom (think of the colourful markings on a tropical fish, the repetition in bird calls or a dolphin's echolocation, and even the patterns in scent), we too rely on pattern for information in order to understand our environment. As we journey through our daily lives our minds are continuously and subconsciously attempting to make order of the things we encounter. We may live increasingly urbanized lives, seemingly far removed from the patterns of the wild, yet we still instinctively respond to and pursue patterns. The cautionary markings on a snakeskin or the white speckles on a poisonous toadstool are mimicked by striped road markings or the raised spots on pavement slabs that signal danger. With at least 80 per cent of the information that our brains receive coming through our eyes, these images tap into our deepest animalistic characteristics. Whether on the African plains or the New York subway, pattern recognition has given us an evolutionary edge that has made humans the survivors that we are.

Going further than simply making sense of our environment, consciously paying attention to the patterns that surround us daily marks the beginning of an exciting journey of discovery that changes the very way we connect to our wider environment. A key principle of PATTERNITY is, as we become more mindful of the world around us, to use this increased awareness to ask bigger questions, to dig beneath the surface of the everyday and take time to understand our place within the bigger picture. As the Austrian-born, American physicist Fritjof Capra (1939–) states in *The Web of Life* (1996): 'The study of pattern is crucial to the understanding of living systems… if we dissect a living organism into its individual parts we lose the pattern and the organism dies.' Pattern reminds us that we are connected to a greater universal tapestry. To understand pattern is to better understand life.

'The kind of attention we bring to bear on the world changes the nature of the world we attend to, the very nature of the world in which those "functions" would be carried out, and in which those "things" would exist. Attention changes what kind of thing comes into being for us: in that way it changes the world.'
The Master and his Emissary: The Divided Brain
and the Making of the Western World (2009),
Iain McGilchrist (1953-), psychiatrist and author

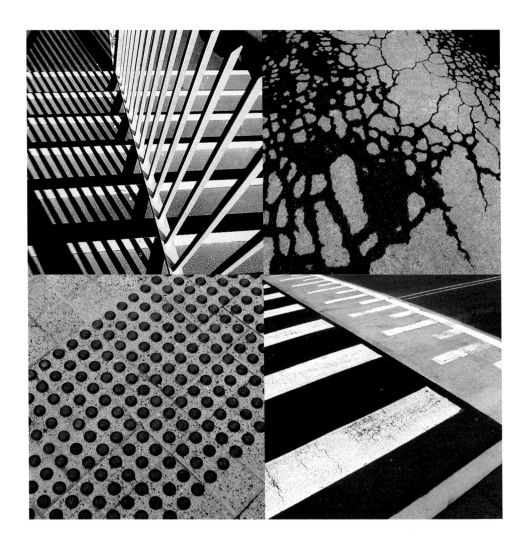

LOOK DOWN

DELIGHT IN DAILY DETAILS

Being aware of pattern can lead to a more positive view of the world and help us to understand our place within it. To delight in the details of the day-to-day is to become more mindful and to live more fully in the present moment. By paying more attention, we begin to open our eyes to a new way of seeing that extends into other areas of our lives.

Top left, Shadow Steps, London | Top right, Crackle Scape, London
Bottom left, Blind Spots, London | Bottom right, Urban Zebra, Sydney

LOOK UP

NOTICE 'NON-PLACES'

Often the best ideas hide in the places we forget to consider: the blind spots that appear throughout our daily lives. However, if we look through the correct lens, even the most mundane of places can inspire and intrigue. Simply *noticing more* breaks the 'autopilot' habit, which so often blinds us to the beauty in the seemingly banal. Slowing down and looking carefully can transform the way we engage with the everyday.

Top left, Scribbled Twigs, Hyde Park, London | Top right, City Drapes, Hong Kong | Bottom left, Holey Façade, Miami | Bottom right, Iron Angles, London

An inner city commute can be a source of inspiration if you make time to notice what you often overlook.

The fleeting beauty of clouds momentarily framed within the metal grid of a tower block.

EXCELLENCE IN THE EVERYDAY | A MINDFUL APPROACH

What does it mean to find beauty in the banal? Why bother to observe the overlooked? In a world of increasing overload, we don't have to retreat to the woods (as American polymath Henry David Thoreau did in the 1850s) to discover 'the essential facts of life'. By immersing himself in nature, Thoreau hoped to gain a more objective understanding of society through personal introspection. But becoming more aware of the world around us is about cultivating a way of seeing that can work in harmony with the challenges of modern life. By simply paying attention, shifting focus and noticing more, daily life can become a visual feast, reminding us of our part amid the vastness of humanity. Noticing a wave of multicoloured wires while we wait for our train to arrive, or spotting a fleeting shadow pass by as we wait in the doctor's surgery are simple ways of experiencing the delicate details of each moment along the way, as opposed to being preoccupied purely with the final destination.

This approach uses pattern as a trigger to bring us back to the present moment. It is our way of stopping to wonder what we might be walking past, to go slowly when we could be going fast, to appreciate the incidental and insignificant. Through this new way of seeing, we can build a more observant way of being, which extends into other aspects of our lives. Being more aware of what is happening in each moment can significantly increase our wellbeing, giving us an important sense of wider perspective and glimmers of gratitude that can often get lost in modern culture. Above all, it means cultivating a more mindful attitude – not being so overwhelmed that we end up missing the magnificent minutiae of our extraordinary existence and the small moments of wonder that collectively make up the rest of our lives.

From day one we wanted to encourage people to develop a more heightened perception of their surroundings in order to spread a message of wider-reaching positive social change. It is a philosophy to which influential figures ranging from Gautama Buddha to the Dalai Lama, Tenzin Gyatso, have dedicated their lives. Lasting happiness derives from living fully in the present and we can use pattern as a catalyst, a trigger, to bring us directly back to the current moment. We can begin to define PATTERNITY as a philosophy of experience. For there is delight in the daily details and we should create space in order to appreciate this – because that combination of air and light will never create the exact formation ever again. To remember this is to remember the transient and supremely precious nature of life.

> *'The present moment is filled with joy and happiness.*
> *If you are attentive, you will see it.'*
> Thích Nhất Hạnh (1926-), Vietnamese Zen Buddhist monk

At PATTERNITY we seek to redefine the basic perception of 'pattern' to something more than a classic polka-dot dress, stretch of wallpaper or swathe of fabric. PATTERNITY is as much about giving equal importance to the mundane as to the magnificent. While we embrace the dazzling art of Bridget Riley or the stylized prints of fashion designer Holly Fulton – which are both easy for the eye to recognize as magnificent demonstrations of pattern implementation – we also aim to showcase one image in

The magnificence of a meticulously stacked supermarket shelf is accessible to all.

Celebrating incidental similarities between Holly Fulton's fashion and everyday flooring.

association with another. Riley's stripes are mirrored in the rows of tinned food on supermarket shelves and Fulton's engineered prints are echoed in bathroom tile formations. There is accessibility in this way of seeing that spreads far beyond the confines of a private art gallery or exclusive fashion show. This is a viewpoint from which boundaries are completely dissolved: what is private becomes public. This way of seeing costs nothing, and when the boundaries between what is mundane and what is magnificent blur, our entire perception of life can shift.

So what do you see when you look out of the window? Whether in the city or countryside, there will be a plethora of patterns both up high and down below. There may be incidental patterns on ceilings, walls or floors; there may be decorative patterns or communicative patterns that guide or inform. There will likely be a convergence of solid and fluid patterns that, upon closer inspection, subtly structure the space in which you currently stand, lie or sit. Often it's not even the details themselves but in the dividing negative space between them where patterns begin to emerge. Look out for diamonds appearing within telegraph poles and wires, or the stretch of sky between two tall buildings. Our everyday experience is not just that of the shapes and forms that surround us but also the spaces in between. As the American poet Leonard Koren (1948–) writes in *Wabi-Sabi: For Artists, Designers, Poets & Philosophers* (1994): '"Greatness" exists in the inconspicuous and overlooked details.' These are the patterns that have the power to remind us of our ultimate impermanence within the greater tapestry of life.

'If the doors of perception were cleansed everything would appear to man as it is, infinite.'

William Blake (1757–1827), Romantic poet, painter and printmaker

PATTERNITY was established with a shared vision. Despite our different backgrounds, upon meeting we realized there were many parallels within our thoughts and research. We had both fastidiously collated a diverse collection of images, not only of fashion, art and design, but also from nature, science, the incidental and the everyday. Our studies combined patterns of both past and present, and we both placed a huge amount of importance on the inspirational power of patterns found in the often overlooked. Spurred by a shared sensitivity and appreciation of repetition, tessellation, periodicity and symmetry, we began to obsessively document them as unique visual references. For us it was about using pattern to achieve balance – to give equal importance to the 'mundane' as to the 'magnificent' and placing them alongside one another in a way that felt natural and democratic. We shared a philosophy of giving pattern a focus tantamount to the end result.

Realizing the power of our combined research and united skills, PATTERNITY very quickly became not only an outlet and archive to consolidate and order all our individual research, but also a place where we could move fluidly between many different disciplines and fields. Seamlessly merging disparate subjects – from honeycomb to an Hermès holdall, from a kitchen sink plughole to a piece of bespoke jewellery, PATTERNITY explores the commonality of pattern in order to define new sequences and connections.

The towering Barbican building near PATTERNITY
STUDIO, London.

A glistening satellite view of Britain,
Ireland and part of Western Europe at night.

DIGITAL DEMOCRACY | INFORMATION EXPLOSION

PATTERNITY first came to being in London's Shoreditch, a stone's throw from the financial hub of the capital and where the commercial and creative communities collide. The concrete cube in which PATTERNITY STUDIO is located sits against a backdrop of totemic metal and steel structures, eternally illuminated against the changing sky. Here, the giant scribble of silver lines that form the London railway system connects the city, and bankers in pinstriped suits jostle with East London's Technicolor artistic tribes in an ebb and flow akin to a scene in Godfrey Reggio's film *Koyaanisqatsi: Life Out of Balance* (1982). A cinematic textile made up of stripes, circles and squares: the seen and the unseen patterns that constitute life.

In the same year that the PATTERNITY archive was launched online, it was announced that there were now more web pages than stars in our galaxy. In less than 25 years the internet has amassed well over a trillion web pages; there is more content uploaded every month than the total sum of books published since the invention of printing five hundred years ago. In early 2015 more than six billion photographs were uploaded to Facebook every month and over four thousand Instagram images every second; the world's sum total of digital information is continuing to grow at a staggering rate. The mass expansion of our cities is now reflected in the glittering digital universe and, in just over two decades, we have created an enormous playground of information and ideas. The world is connected like never before.

Our world has consistently been transformed by similar radical advances, from the construction of the first widely used alphabet by the Phoenicians in the 15th century BC to the invention of movable type by the Chinese craftsman Bi Sheng in the 11th century. Throughout human history, such developments have expanded our minds and enhanced our appreciation and understanding of the world around us. Technology aids our learning and our communication, spreading new ideas and innovations quickly and widely. We're sharing more now than we ever have before, and passing on information has become an inextricable part of life. The internet has not only become a vehicle for conversation but also a whole new medium in its own right. It is a way of life that feels as much a part of us as we are a part of it. The democracy of the digital space has opened up a whole new platform loaded with countless opportunities for creators and curators around the world.

The internet's influence on creativity exploded in the late 1990s with the advent of web publishing tools that facilitated the posting of content by non-technical users. Sites such as WordPress and later Tumblr have helped to democratize self-publishing and the 'blog' has become part of our common language. Suddenly the screen was being treated as the printed page. This, together with the improvements to software and hardware (such as the lenses on cameras and phones to the autocorrect function on our computers), has helped to create a new form of media. Bloggers began to take prime positions in the front rows of fashion shows alongside long-established editors. Musicians and singers who were unsigned and unseen took to YouTube and began competing with well-known artists.

A blogger at New York Fashion Week stands simultaneously behind and in front of the lens.

Micrograph and drain cover unite the macro with the micro and the mundane with the magnificent.

Free from the restrictions of the hierarchy that traditionally cosseted the arts, passionate amateurs and emerging talents, such as the fashion writer and editor Tavi Gevinson, who came to public attention at the age of 12 with her blog *Style Rookie*, were given the autonomy to curate and share their ideas. Soon, the rookies would go on to establish a core following, weaving a web of influence across what had previously been a largely impenetrable domain. With the floodgates well and truly open, there were endless opportunities for those with a defined niche to find their voice. *The Sartorialist,* for example, was established online in 2005 by photographer Scott Schuman, and has since gone on to become the blueprint for street style and street fashion photography today.

No longer was being creatively conscious limited to living in a major city – the internet has become a universe of endless inspiration, bringing together little-known ideas from the past and the present as well as providing tantalizing glimpses of the future. Whether via smart phone, tablet or public library, virtually anyone, anywhere is able to take inspiration. A world with Facebook, Twitter, Instagram, Blogspot, Pinterest, WordPress and Tumblr has, in many ways, helped to establish a sense of belonging to an entire generation. We are spiders sitting in a glistening web of global communication.

'It's like watching the planet develop a nervous system. The ability to collect, analyze, triangulate, and visualize vast amounts of data in real time is something the human race has never had before.'
Rick Smolan (1949–), photographer and author

However, we are only beginning to learn how to balance the immense opportunities for knowledge and communication that we hold in our fingertips. In this infinite web of scrolling, transitory newsfeeds, headlines, photographs and video content, the need for a certain kind of digital contemplation has become all the more crucial. We have always needed gatekeepers to simplify, edit and control the quality and quantity of the information we consume. In the past this has taken the form of editors, educators and institutions, but with no grand editor-in-chief, principal or managing director of the internet we're in the midst of information overload – something that is reflected as much in the digital sphere as it is in our physical culture. With no guidebook on how to navigate this online world, there is an increasing need for places reserved for digital meditation and contemplation.

REORDERING ONLINE CHAOS | CURATING COINCIDENCES

PATTERNITY could only have happened at this time of newfound digital democracy. Our intention was to create a quiet digital space amid the clutter by choosing to focus on just one thing: pattern. We also wanted to establish this search for pattern through a very selective and mindful lens. We would bring together many different worlds of inspiration – from fashion to food, architecture to art, science to space and beyond. PATTERNITY is a simple idea underpinned by a strong social mission to explore the positive power of pattern to better understand life.

LOOK AROUND

OBSERVE THE OVERLOOKED

In a world overloaded with stimulation, observing pattern can help to make sense of the chaos. Pattern has the power to make us more mindful and more engaged with the everyday. Often it's not the 'things' themselves that offer the most inspiration, but the spaces in between them. These are the patterns that, in our hurry to get from A to B, we often overlook. Yet to miss these is, in some ways, to miss everything.

Top left, Brick Bundle, London | Top right, Tyre Tetris, London | Bottom left, Seat Repeat, Australia | Bottom right, Tidal Jack Stack, Corsica

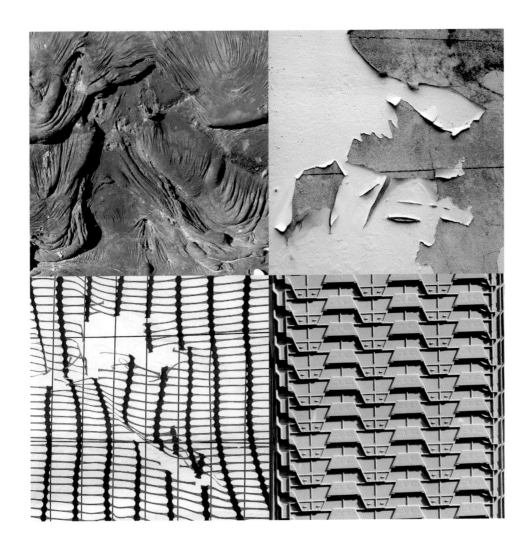

NOTICE MORE

ENJOY EVERYDAY EXCELLENCE

Allowing ourselves to take more enjoyment in the moment can shift our perspective of the world around us. Excellence is everywhere, from the fleeting shadows cast through railings onto the pavement below, to the reflections projected on the high-rise architecture above our heads. To notice these fleeting occurrences is to remember the impermanence of humanity and our place within a much bigger picture.

Top left, Tarmac Wrinkles, London | Top right, Paint Peels, Australia
Bottom left, Broken Links, Berlin | Bottom right, Crate Collection, New York

Pattern inspiration + curation

Seeing pattern everywhere - from the mundane to the magnificent

READ MORE

STRIPE STRIDE | MARC JACOBS SS13
#LINE   #SS13   #MONOCHROME
#DRESS   #FASHION
23.02.15

SECURITY SHADOW | PATTERNITY
#URBAN   #STREET   #LINE   #SHADOW
#STRIPE   #GREY
13.06.12

A stripe story showcased on the PATTERNITY image archive.

We wanted to create an online destination that would establish a new vocabulary, presenting patterns from everyday life in a way that would engage and inspire. Through our archive we began to organize the infinite variety of the patterns that surround everyone everywhere. From the outset, we saw PATTERNITY as a giant, anonymous filter, sifting through the four corners of the digital and physical worlds to select only the very best pattern inspiration – with no stone left unturned in the quest. Most importantly, we wanted to encourage people to look at the world around them differently, with a heightened awareness and appreciation of their surroundings.

'There is a phenomenon which we are forced to communicate: simply, to teach how to see.'
César Manrique (1919–1992), Spanish artist, architect and activist

Recognizing the importance of the PATTERNITY digital archive, we strive to preserve the past and present in a way that is easy to revisit and reappropriate. In an age where Google can lead us straight from Socrates to the Spice Girls, the archiving of imagery into an effective and considered order felt increasingly vital. Our research, which fastidiously collates the most inspiring patterns from all over the digital universe in one place, is organized primarily by its pattern, but secondarily by other subcategories such as material, location, era and originator. In essence, we are building a new universe grounded by the unique power of the human mind to see and create relationships and recognize patterns, merged with the power of computer software that helps to create a powerful system of organization.

A search for 'stripes' in the PATTERNITY archive might result in a piece of clothing by American designer Marc Jacobs, alongside an incidental arrangement of supermarket shopping trolleys, a photograph of a shadow taken by one of our global network of Instagrammers, and the steel, aluminium and Perspex stacks that make up American artist Donald Judd's *Untitled* (1980). Generating new and inspiring connections between seemingly disparate subjects, these internal searches then become PATTERNITY 'stories' where the worlds of pattern and their many permutations collide. This bringing together of patterns requires a consideration of visual coincidences; we can disregard what something is made of and instead join Gregory Bateson and consider what its common properties and relationships are, asking above all else, 'What is its pattern?'

The PATTERNITY pattern archive is as much about inspiring creativity in others as it is about encouraging them to simply notice more. Our image archive has influenced some of the world's most respected designers, serving as the essential destination for research by brands including Vivienne Westwood, Chanel, Céline, Foster + Partners, Volkswagen and Nike. Their subscriptions provide the lifeblood of the PATTERNITY organization, which in turn enables us to work on our many pattern-focused educational projects. These programmes are at the heart of everything we do, bringing us full-circle to the original PATTERNITY mission to explore and exalt the positive power of pattern.

From spider's webs to smashed screens, pay attention to the coincidences that abound.

The PATTERNITY way of seeing began with the documentation of bold geometric shapes.

'Rather than a materialist, I would prefer to consider myself a "patternist".
It's through the emergent powers of the pattern that we transcend.'
Ray Kurzweil (1948–), author, inventor and director
of engineering at Google

We have always positioned PATTERNITY as a positive reaction to a very paradoxical point in time. The ordering of chaos, either visual or theoretical, can establish a comforting presence and PATTERNITY.ORG reorganizes a world of endless inspiration. Although we never look to current trends, the archive has subsequently evolved to become a unique and unparalleled record of time and culture through pattern. The ever-expanding PATTERNITY archive of imagery both online at PATTERNITY.ORG and offline housed within the PATTERNITY server doesn't just showcase the infinitely inspiring presence of pattern, it uses pattern to put a world of abundance into order and serves as a catalyst for others to pay more attention to the world around them.

The PATTERNITY approach is one of 'inclusive exclusivity'. In order to pair a seemingly unremarkable brick wall with a microscopic image of termites building a colony, it is necessary to disregard the context of what you are looking at. The skills, techniques and ethos of a recent fashion graduate sit next to those of someone long forgotten or unknown. Sparking curiosity is at the heart of the PATTERNITY approach and the image archive began with easily recognizable imagery that triggered new questions: how much does a smashed car window reflect a frosted spider's web? How does that discarded electrical tubing mirror the latest collection by fashion designer Iris van Herpen? The research we collate and organize is as much about the latest catwalk creations in Paris or contemporary sculptures at Frieze art fair as it is about crystal formations dating back millions of years or the microscopic patterns of DNA in the cells deep within our own bodies.

'All things come into being by conflict of opposites.'
Heraclitus (535–475BC), Pre-Socratic Greek philosopher

THE SHAPES THAT SURROUND US | FAMILIAR FORMS

At PATTERNITY we have always been greatly influenced by the patterns and shapes that construct our everyday man-made surroundings. Most of our early 'stories' referenced the many patterns found within bold geometric structures, everyday design details, bold monochrome fashion and graphic design, and blocky interior and exterior architectural details. Our priority was the fundamental forms mainly within the urban environment reflecting our own localities and interests. From the beginning we have referred to this as a focus on 'the building blocks of life': the simple circles, triangles, squares and polygons that make up our everyday environments. These bold man-made patterns are still very much synonymous with the PATTERNITY aesthetic seen today within much of our photographic work, design collaborations and creative direction.

Pattern inspiration as documented on
PATTERNITRIPS from London (above) to
Hong Kong (opposite) to Sydney (below),
all aiming to inspire a more positive
connection with our urban environments.

The fundamental drive at PATTERNITY is to encourage people to use pattern as a kind of language: a tool to reconnect the dots in an increasingly disconnected world. Computers are the first truly universal medium, but they are only the beginning of the story. Having stamped the PATTERNITY visual aesthetic online, it became increasingly important for us to take the PATTERNITY mission out of the digital space and into the real world. Shortly after launching the image archive we began running photographic PATTERNITRIPS, where we lead groups around everyday areas of cities encouraging participants to document the patterns that they might usually walk past. We set about encouraging local groups – both big and small, young and old – to pay attention to, and seek inspiration from, the very last places they might look.

One tour challenged a group of teenagers from East London to take to their local neighbourhoods and 'find beauty in the boring'. Scouring car parks, train stations and traffic jams, participants excitedly returned with images of spectacularly stacked cardboard boxes, twisting telephone wires and colourful crumbling paintwork. The project encouraged them to see their surroundings with a fresh set of eyes – to see how much inspiration there is, if we can only look with focus and increased awareness. The search for pattern has the power to positively shift the perception of our surroundings, and in a seemingly enduring way – as one member of the group said when contacting the studio weeks later, 'Now I see patterns everywhere I go and it makes me really happy'.

Encouraging individuals to look up, look down and all around them with an attuned eye invites them to pay full attention, as if seeing their surroundings for the very first time. With this newfound clarity, higher consciousness and with equal measures of creativity and curiosity, we can engage with the real world with a child-like inquisitiveness once again. We need to re-activate our innate awareness, to open our eyes and see our surroundings anew.

Inspiration is everywhere and to be inspired costs nothing.

'All the effort in the world won't matter if you're not inspired.'
Chuck Palahniuk (1962-), American novelist and freelance journalist

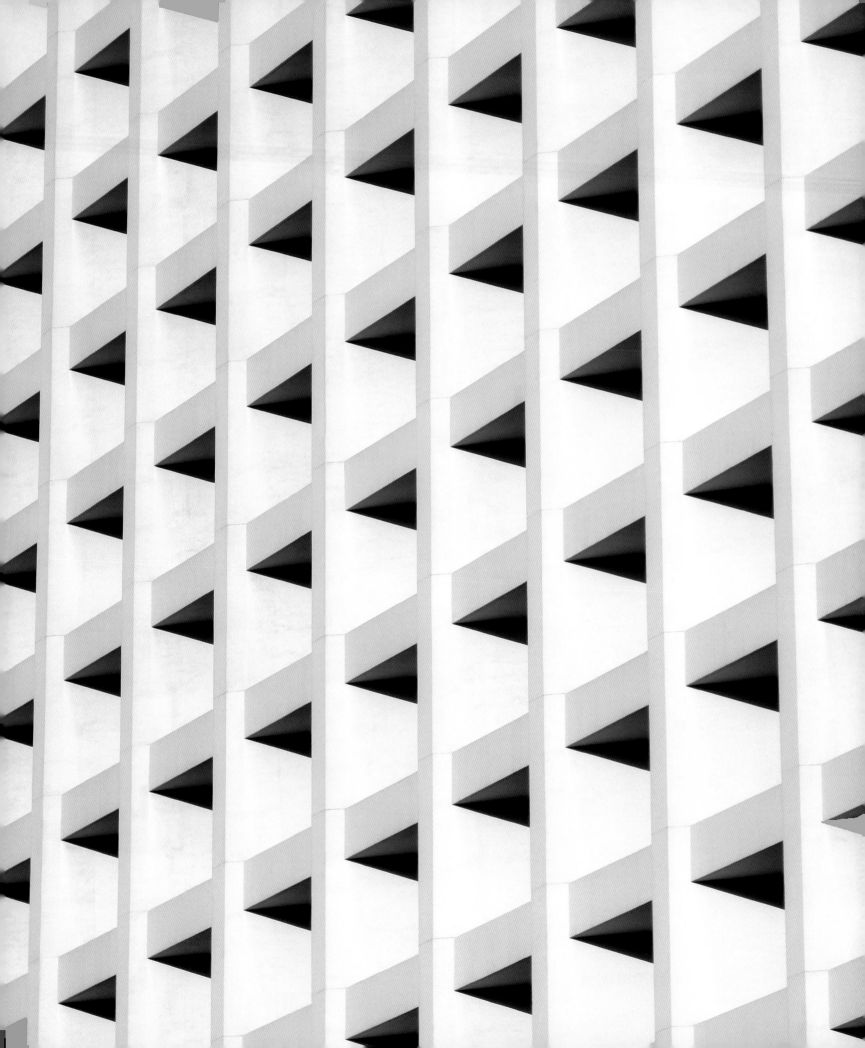

Pages 46–7, Balcony Bends, Kane Hulse, Cuba

Left, Step and Repeat, PATTERNITY, Wimbledon AELTC, London | Right, Verdant Verticals, Gustavo Zylbersztajn, fashion: Dolce & Gabbana, sunglasses: Anna-Karin Karlsson

'There is a phenomenon which we are forced to communicate: simply, to teach how to see.'

César Manrique (1919–1992), Spanish artist, architect and activist

PATTERN FOCUS

#LINE #STRIPE #STACK #STEP #REPEAT

The binary nature of stripes – creating positive and negative space – has been exploited in modern day technology by magnetic strips in credit cards and barcodes on every product for sale, denoting unique information that can be processed in an instant.

The simplicity of the stripe is also a qualifier of uniqueness: stripes, whether brash or elegant, can reflect a membership or exclusion to some moral or ethical code. Whether seen in the thick black bars behind which we place criminals, or the identifying stripes of sports teams and flags, we tend to use stripes to draw attention to who is in or who is out.

Pejorative stripes (those that diminish the wearer's status) originate from the Middle Ages. Stripes were relegated to outcasts, such as prostitutes, madmen and clowns, and communicated discordance with accepted values of the right or wrong way of being.

Monochrome stripes seen in nature are just as conspicuous. Zebra markings are more functional than symbolic, with scientists suggesting their purposes being to assist in temperature regulation and insect repellence. Many have also cited the stripes as aiding in more primal survival techniques, allowing quick recognition between friend or foe and creating dazzling visual effects that confuse approaching predators.

The stripe serves to add character and identity, be it to the Breton sailor or the unassuming clownfish.

Top left, Stripe Tease, Willem Jaspert, dress: Danielle Scutt | Top right, Ascending Angles, Sydney Opera House | Middle left, Bridge Bars, Brazil | Middle right, Multi-storey Stripe, Hong Kong Bottom left, Sun Stacks, Croatia | Bottom right, Line Order, Federal District, Mexico City

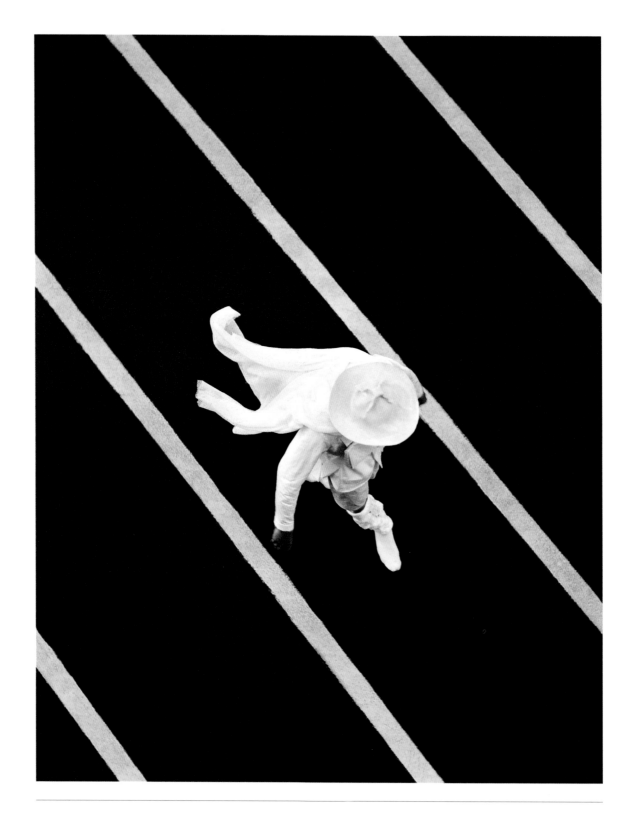

Lane Lines, Rory van Millingen, fashion: Kiko Kostadinov

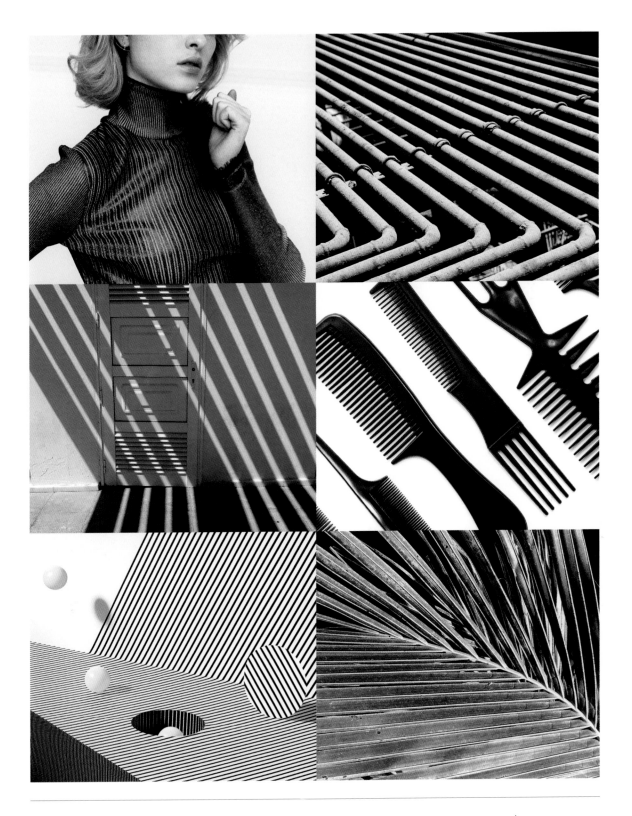

Top left, Stripe Stretch, fashion: vintage | Top right, Pipe Corner, Beijing | Middle left, Shifting Shadows, Lanzarote | Middle right, Comb Teeth, PATTERN POWER — Superstripe Series Bottom left, Stripe in One, 'Stripes and Dots' Series | Bottom right, Palm Pleats, Ibiza

Left, Lighthouse Levels, Ed Gilligan, Dungeness, England | Right, Leggy Lines, Georges Antoni

'Opposites define one another and bring each other into existence.'

Iain McGilchrist (1953–), psychiatrist and author

∞ CAMOUFLAGE REIMAGINED

THE 'FLEET OF DAZZLE' | COLLABORATION

We were approached by Imperial War Museums to develop the 'Fleet of Dazzle' (right), a range of monochrome products that repositioned the iconic 'dazzle' camouflage patterns painted to disguise and protect ships during World War I. This first collection was part of a larger-scale collaboration with Imperial War Museums to coincide with World War I Centenary commemorations in 2014. The collection celebrated the power of pattern to protect and unite at a time of intense conflict.

▶ THE PATTERNS THAT SHAPE HISTORY

PATTERN.CONFLICT.UNITY | FILM

We joined forces with film-maker and fashion features director of *POP* magazine, Lily Silverton, to create a short film (below). Uniting naval archive footage from both World Wars I and II with new studio footage of our Imperial War Museums collaboration, *Pattern.Conflict.Unity* tells the unique story of 'dazzle' camouflage beneath the surface.

Pages 58–9, Library Portal, Nicolas Stjernström Nielsen, Phillips Exeter Academy Library, USA

Left, Concrete Circles, PATTERNITY, London | Right, Ring of Beauty, Straulino

'The present moment is filled with joy and happiness. If you are attentive, you will see it.'

Thích Nhất Hạnh (1926–), Vietnamese zen Buddhist monk, teacher, author, poet and peace activist

◆ MARVELLING THE MUNDANE

▶ EVERYDAY EXCELLENCE | INSTALLATION

We created a series of installations and animations for Swedish retailer COS to celebrate abstraction in everyday life. The project was inspired by the serendipitous spectacles that surround us everywhere we go. The repeated, symmetrical and precise presentation of our installation drew attention to the subtle and unexpected details found in familiar places and on everyday objects. Our aim was to encourage a shift in focus, changing the perception of the omnipresent and often overlooked.

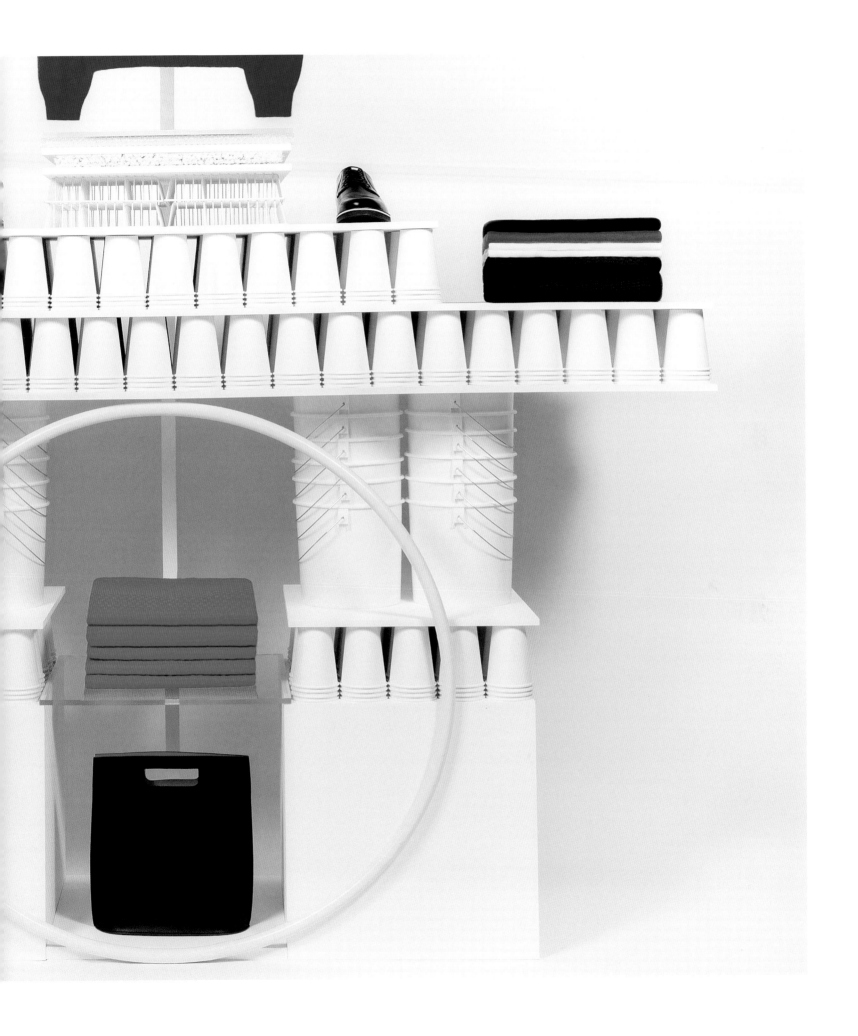

PATTERN FOCUS

#CIRCLE #HOOP #HOLE #RING #CURVE

The circle in its varying forms is perhaps the most timeless of shapes in the natural world, from the magnificence of the sun to the tiny bubble-like spots of frogspawn.

In Hindu cosmology the circle is symbolic of earth, one of the four elements, and is given feminine characteristics, while in Greek philosophy it is emblematic of masculinity, representing movement and activity. The prolific use of the circle in cosmological imagery across different religions and philosophies, from the Christian halo to the Buddhist wheel of life, demonstrates that the circle is a highly mercurial shape.

Elegant and perfect, the circle's balance is elusive across its natural or man-made manifestations. The circle is aesthetically and practically functional. Whether as the plate on your table or the bull's-eye of a target, the circle presents a dualism between symmetry and beauty, wholeness and exclusivity. But circles can be highly exclusionary too. Spots can be nature's way of warning against an antigen that you are carrying, or they can offer a means of safety and camouflage for animals living in the dappled light of forests.

We can adopt circles as forms of inclusion, whether as the dinner tables that we sit around or the moral balances to which we subscribe to create our particular versions of 'wholeness' or 'roundedness'. The circle's ability to express equality as well as unity using elaborated social and moral codes makes it a supreme icon of the continuities of life.

Top left, Hole Style, New York | Top right, Shadow Hoops, Doboj, Bosnia | Middle left, Round Reflections, glass on paper | Middle right, Sun Drain, New York | Bottom left, Lobe Loop, COOPS London | Bottom right, Curve and Curl, veneer and mirror

Left, Office Spots, PATTERNITY, Hong Kong | Right, Holes and Corners, Sarah Piantadosi, cashmere jumper, grid trousers and circle jersey: PATTERNITY ∞ Chinti + Parker

'All the effort in the world won't matter if you're not inspired.'

Chuck Palahniuk (1962–), American novelist and freelance journalist

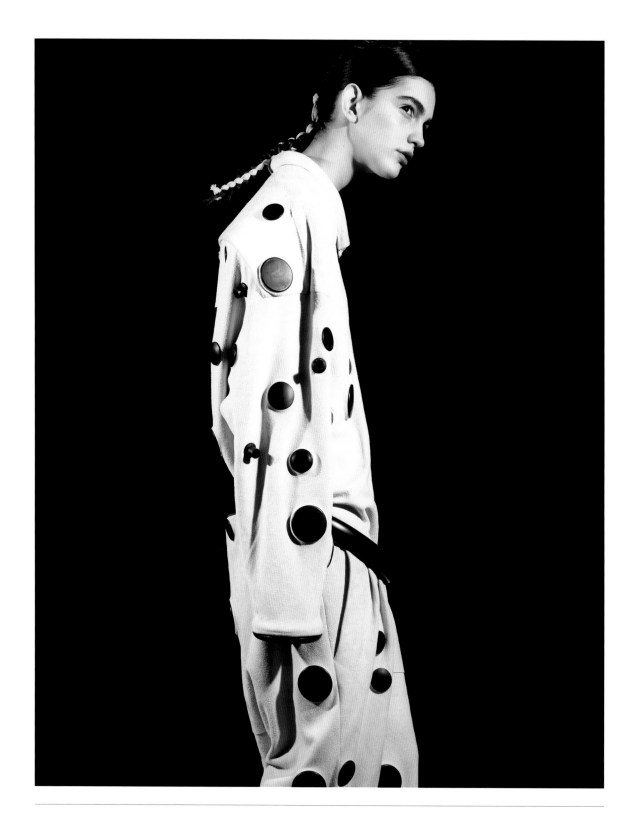

Black Spot, Amy Gwatkin, fashion: Malene List Thomsen

Top left, Dalmatian Duo, Scott Trindle, fashion: Joseph Turvey | Top right, Parasol Pipes, Nigeria | Middle left, Cup Crowd, PATTERNITY STUDIO | Middle right, Satellite Spots, Nigeria Bottom left, Seat Circles, Ibiza | Bottom right, Drainage Dots, San Francisco

∞ CELEBRATING THE BUILDING BLOCKS OF LIFE

DESERT PATTERN | SHOE COLLABORATION

Working with established products allows us to create something greater than the sum of its parts. Our unisex desert boot collaboration with iconic British footwear brand Clarks Originals (right) gave a new dimension and meaning that went beyond the surface. We wanted to explore the power of contrasts reflected in the bold rearrangements of circles, lines, triangles and squares. Our aim – to strike an interesting balance between male/female, light/dark, hard/soft, shiny/matte – was reflected in the pattern. It resulted in a stylized reinterpretation of the fundamental shapes that surround us all everywhere we go.

▶ A JOURNEY THROUGH PATTERN

PATTERN PIONEERS | FILM PROJECT

Collaborating further with Clarks Originals, we conceived and produced a film that would depict the story of desert explorer Nathan Clark, who, inspired by the footwear of off-duty army officers in Cairo's fabled old bazaar, designed the first desert boot in 1949. The film (below) is divided into three distinct parts, taking the viewer on a journey of inspiration, exploration and innovation from the past, through the present and into the future.

Pages 72–3, Check and Step, PATERNITY, London

Left, Warped Wire, Teddy Cohen, Tel Aviv, Israel | Right, Net Wrap, Niklas Hoejlund, sports netting

'Pattern is much more embedded into the fabric of our universe than we ever thought.'

Andrea Sella, professor of inorganic chemistry, University College London

PATTERN FOCUS

#SQUARE #GRID #NET #TILE #CUBE

The square has traditionally been employed to communicate and reinforce ideas of modernity, homogeneity and scientific methods of meaning across modern life. Frames help to compartmentalize objects and grids formalize the urban environment, aiding navigation and maximizing the use of space. Nowhere is the square more clearly employed as a symbol of modern civilization than in a town square: a public space that was created for political mediation and social interaction.

Squares have also helped in making knowledge of political and geographic structures more clear. From the tiny pixel squares used in digital communication to the grids and plans used in the planning and constructing of urban geographies, squares have been intrinsic to providing comprehensive overviews of large areas of information for quick and effective consumption and navigation. Squares are everywhere.

Squares also disrupt the lucidity of an environment, creating a visual noise that is instantly recognizable. In the UK there is perhaps no stronger presence of the square than the chequered patterns applied to police uniforms and transport, reflecting the arresting powers of the patterned square.

The square also holds a deeply pacifying quality. It addresses Modernist desires for honest functionality. With their neutrality and unifying qualities, the square and the right angle have served both the Dutch painter Piet Mondrian and the influential German-American architect Ludwig Mies van der Rohe in their minimalist principles.

Top left, Checker Out, Julia Kennedy, fashion: Louise Alsop | Top right, Grey Grids, Nigeria
Middle left, Square Squared, glass mosaic tiles | Middle right, Shadow Corner, Nottingham,
England | Bottom left, Tilted Tiles, cast metal tiles | Bottom right, Grid Glasses, sunglasses:
LARKE X DARKROOM

Left, Bending Bin, PATTERNITY, Croatia | Right, Lattice Legs, Jamie Morgan

'The chessboard is the world, the pieces are the phenomena of the universe, and the rules of the game are what we call the laws of nature.'

Thomas Henry Huxley (1825-1895), biologist

▶ BRINGING THE OVERLOOKED TO LIFE

CITY SHAPES | ANIMATION

This special moving-image project (below), commissioned by YCN, was produced in collaboration with animation studio Plastic Horse and aimed to bring the PATTERNITY image archive to life. Our photographic documentation of 'non-places' converges and collides as animated repetition, optical transitions and warped perspectives abstract the imagery. Set to generic sounds of the everyday city streets, the resulting animation served as a beautiful and simple kaleidoscopic reminder that inspiration lies in the many areas we tend to overlook.

Above, Grid Disguise, Marlen Keller, digital projection

Top left, Catwalk Cut Out, fashion: Balmain | Top right, Cyan City, London | Middle left,
Crossing Clouds, New York | Middle right, Puffy Pouches | Bottom left, Seat Layer, Edinburgh
Bottom right, Solar Panel Pile, Goa, India

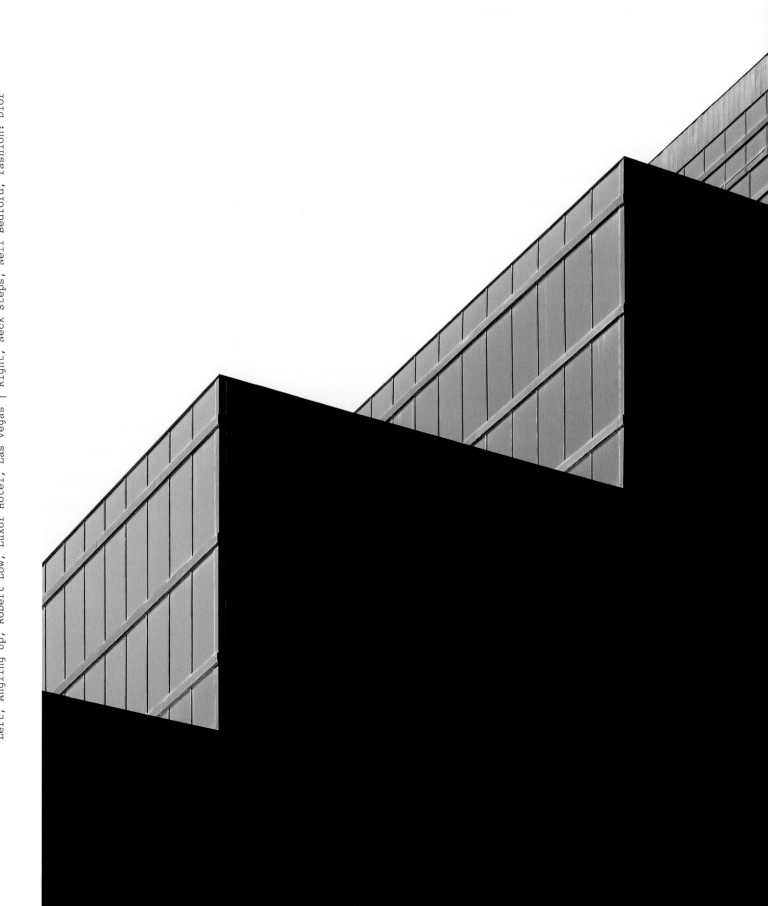

Pages 84–5, Zig-Zag Zone, PATTERNITY, Kerala, India

Left, Angling Up, Robert Low, Luxor Hotel, Las Vegas | Right, Neck Steps, Neil Bedford, fashion: Dior

'The searching-out and thorough investigation of truth ought to be the primary study of man.'

Marcus Tullius Cicero (106–43BC), Roman philosopher, political theorist and consul

PATTERN FOCUS

#TRIANGLE #ZIGZAG #PYRAMID

Although the triangle is the rarest of all naturally occurring shapes, it can be spotted in a few specific circumstances. Triangles help to create some of the strongest natural forms – whether in the configuration of a spider's web or in the greatly magnified structure of a diamond – and are remarkable for being able to sustain and respond to incredibly high pressures and forces placed upon them.

In 1912, for example, a Norwegian by the name of Jens Eriksen designed and constructed a special fish rack in the shape of a triangle, which made it possible to evenly distribute large quantities of fish onto the racks for drying, revolutionizing the fishing industry at the time. As more modern examples, the common shape of cable suspension bridges and the frame of a bicycle also demonstrate the balance and distribution of force to which the triangle can give rise.

Unlike squares, which can fold under pressure, a triangle can transfer pressure and force from one side to the two others. As a result, the only means of cutting through a diamond is achieved through a combination of extremely high momentum and force. In the same way, it is the triangular facets of pyramids that make them so strong and enduring – as exemplified by the structural longevity of the Egyptian pyramids at Giza. The pyramid shape can be found all around us too. It has influenced our environment in myriad subtle ways, from dress and skirt shapes to church spires and even rocket components.

Top left, Cheese Wedge, Gorgonzola | Top right, Wrapped Railings, Bristol, England
Middle left, Boat Point, Tel Aviv, Israel | Middle right, Tarmac Triangles, Milan, Italy
Bottom left, Concrete Cuts, Hong Kong | Bottom right, Pyramid Peaks, Giza, Egypt

∞ MARQUETRY CRAFT REVISITED

SHIFT TABLE | BESPOKE FURNITURE

Our furniture projects with marquetry specialist Toby Winteringham demonstrate how considered pattern application can bring renewed aesthetic and interest to the traditional expectations of hand-rendered craft techniques. The pattern represents the shifting of time, the moving of light and dark, and the process of cutting out and filling in. Pieces from the 'Shift' collection earned a *Wallpaper** Design Award in 2011 and led to several bespoke luxury interior commissions, including a north London synagogue, retail space in Dubai and government offices in Zagreb. The bold pattern design moved away from the intricate designs synonymous with the Ancient Chinese craft and represents a timely demonstration of the power of pattern to draw attention to and revive traditional methods and materials.

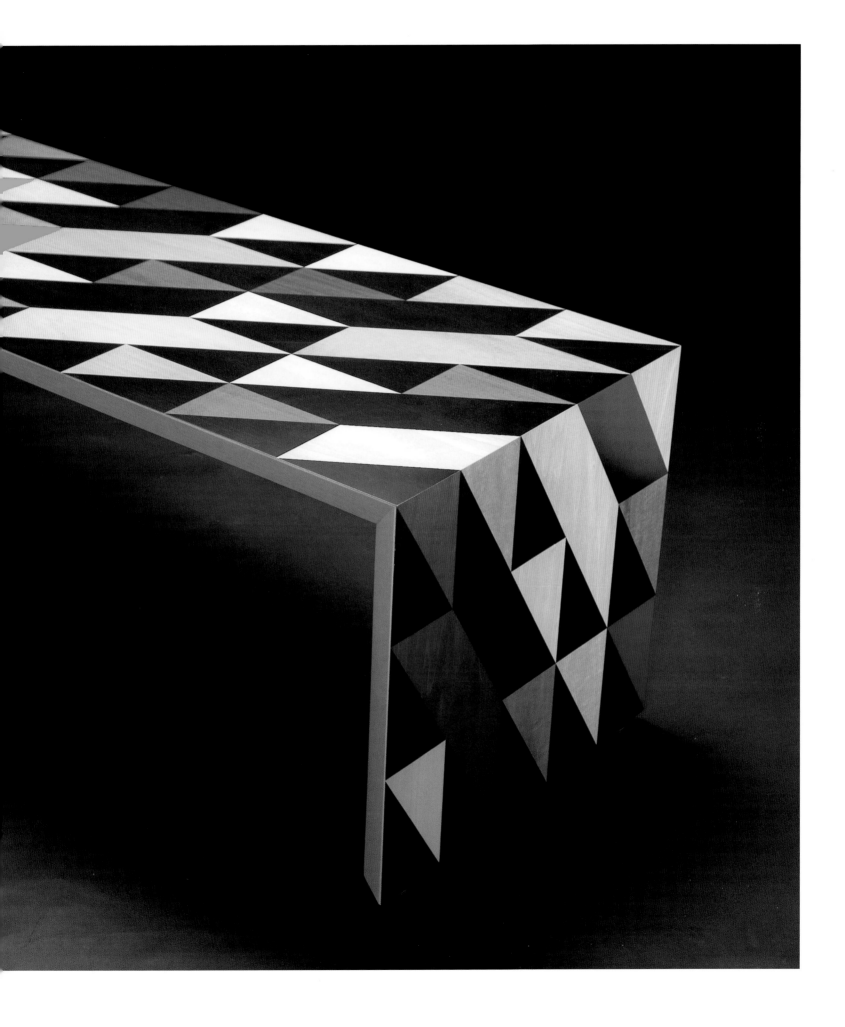

Above, Angle Pose, Andrew Yee, fashion: Hannah Marshall

Top left, Jagged Jacket, Willem Jaspert, fashion: Martina Spetlova | Top right, Zip Up, metal zip | Middle left, Chevron Shadows, Sydney | Middle right, Tacking Tiles, Hong Kong Bottom left, Bridge Bend, Maria Pia Bridge, Portugal | Bottom right, Two Tone Tablet, marble

Left, Car Park Crosses, PATERNITY, Hong Kong | Right, Facet Jacket, Brendan Freeman, jacket: Issey Miyake

'Geometry is knowledge of the eternally existent.'

Plato (c.427–348 bc), philosopher and mathematician

Pages 98—9, Viewpoint, Neil Watson,
Barbican, London

∞ CONSCIOUS CLOTH MEETS CONSCIOUS PATTERN

ETHICAL KNITWEAR | REWORKED

Our 'Conscious Cloth Meets Conscious Pattern' project (right and below), produced in collaboration with ethical knitwear specialists Chinti and Parker, looked to urban architecture and everyday details for inspiration. We used photographs from our many PATTERNITRIPS around the globe as creative starting points, and combined our bold geometric patterns with Chinti and Parker's timeless designs and commitment to sustainable style. The resulting 28-piece collection is a wearable celebration of pattern and its inspiring presence within our everyday environments.

▶ PATTERN BENEATH THE SURFACE

CONSCIOUS PATTERN | FILM PROJECT

PATTERNITY is involved in concepts that arise from 'visual' patterns, encouraging a more mindful way of 'seeing'. This also carries over into patterns that are less obvious. Take for example patterns of behaviour; it is impossible to speak about 'consciousness' without considering sustainability. How things are made and the impact this has on the world around us. Our 'Conscious Pattern' film (below), made in collaboration with British fashion film director Zoe Hitchen, aimed to dig beneath the surface and champion more 'conscious' choices when it comes to our patterns of consumption.

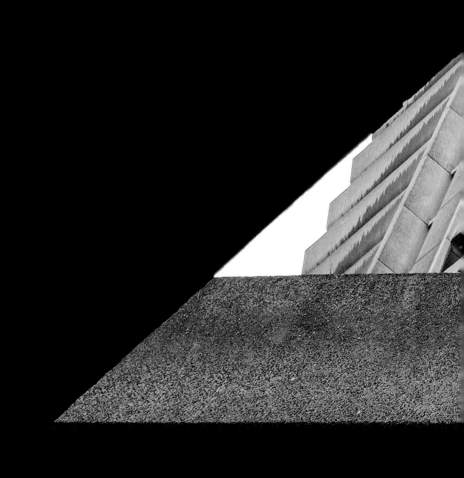

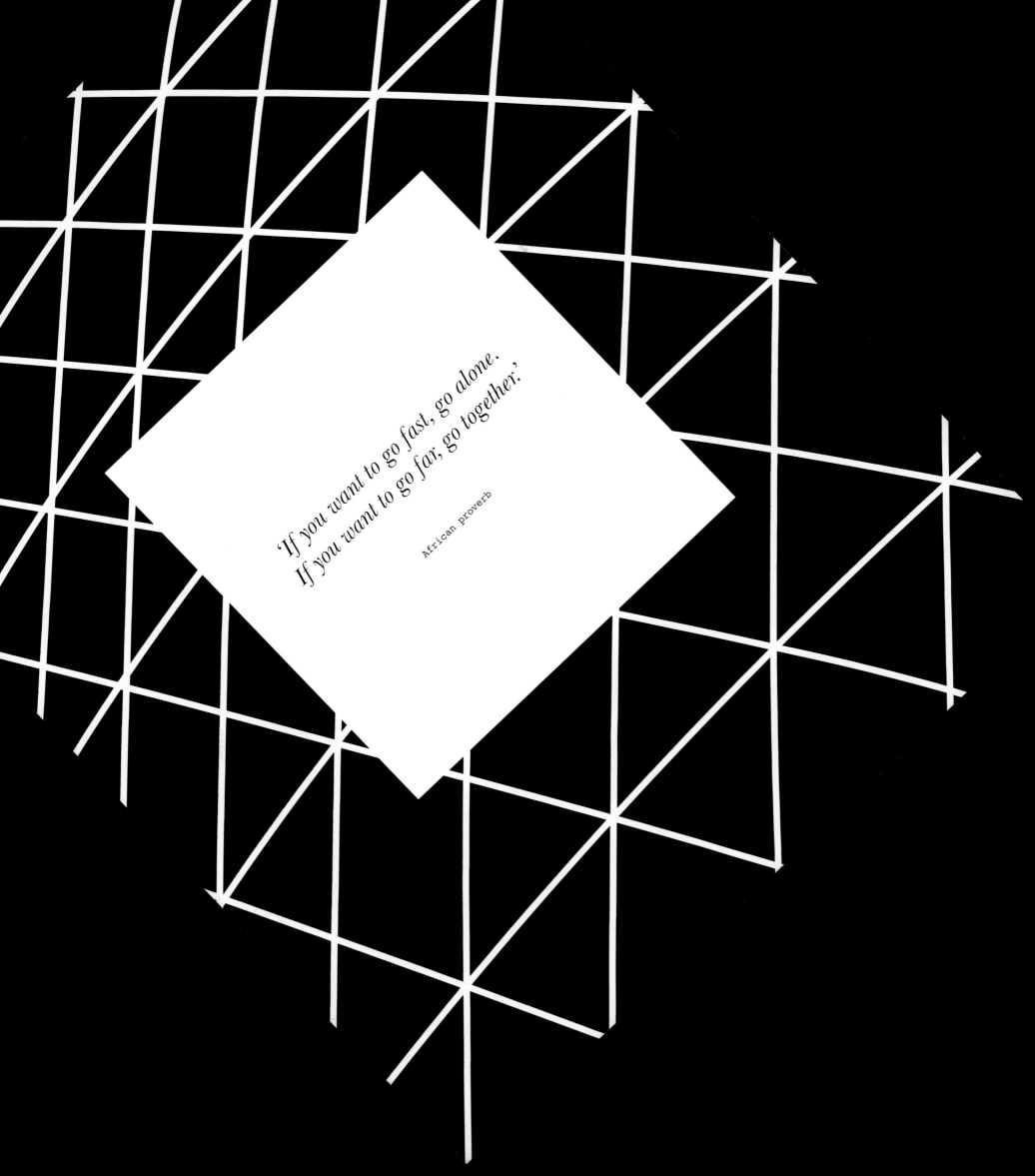

'If you want to go fast, go alone.
If you want to go far, go together.'

African proverb

PART TWO

COLLABORATION

INNOVATION | WHERE CONCEPT
+ CRAFT COLLIDE

Left, Blind Beams, PATTERNITY, London | Right, Passing Phase, PATTERNITY ∞ Toby Winteringham, bureau

'All things are filled full of signs, and it is a wise man who can learn about one thing from another.'

Plotinus (AD205–270), Roman Neo-Platonist philosopher

Left, Corner Tile, PATTERNITY, London | Right, Bricking It, Neil Watson, tights: PATTERNITY

'Nothing ever exists entirely alone; everything is in relation to everything else.'

Gautama Buddha (c.563–483BC)

Left, Top Tiers, JTB Photo, Nyatapola Temple, Nepal | Right, Rugged Repeat, PATTERNITY ∞ Made by Node, hand-woven Tibetan wool

'The great use of life is to spend it for something that will outlast it.'

William James (1842–1910), philosopher and psychologist

Left, Dazzle Ship, Surgeon Oscar Parkes, World War I | Right, Dazzle Pattern, PATTERNITY ∞ Imperial War Museums, Fleet of Dazzle cushion

'Men must be aware of the wisdom and the strength that is in them if their understanding is to be expanded.'

Luc de Clapiers, Marquis de Vauvenargues (1715–1747), French soldier, moralist

Designer Max Lamb's multicoloured engineered marble skillfully balances tradition with Modernism.

Page 110—11, Stretched Skin, Bart Hess, 'Mutants' Series.

Artist Shelley James regularly collaborates with scientists, exploring the intersection between material and virtual space.

THE POWER OF COLLABORATION | JOINING THE DOTS

Historically speaking, many of the world's most important creative innovations have been brought about by small and close-knit groups working in relative isolation. Take, for example, the circle of influential English writers, intellectuals, philosophers and artists that would come to be known as the Bloomsbury Group in the first half of the 20th century, or the creative minds that kicked-off the British punk movement in the mid-1970s. From Virginia Woolf and Vanessa Bell to Malcolm McLaren and Vivienne Westwood, creative communities and radical ideas seemed to be born from the collaborations of intimately linked and similarly inspired artists and craftspeople.

However, in today's digital age, with its abundance of social networks and keenly connected institutions, a newfound dialogue has been established between what were previously segregated specialisms. This rise of cross-disciplinary collaboration is one of the most defining creative developments since the late 1990s. As the worlds of art, fashion and design have merged, other disciplines, from mathematics and music, architecture and anthropology, biology and beyond, have also been busy blurring their boundaries. Today the opportunity to experiment with material, concept and craftsmanship has never been more available. Individuals, brands and corporations alike have a new playground in which to cross-pollinate and learn from each other. And it is through this merging of fields that we can begin to feed our curiosities, tap into the resources of other disciplines and create outcomes far greater than the sum of their individual parts.

> *'Creativity involves breaking out of established patterns*
> *in order to look at things in a different way.'*
> Edward de Bono (1933—), author, physician and inventor

Prestigious publications such as *Wallpaper** – which has been running its annual *Wallpaper** Handmade project since 2010 – strives to bring these kinds of creative collaborations to the fore by presenting a global community of artists, designers, craftspeople and manufacturers with the challenge to produce unique furniture, fittings, fashion, foodstuffs and more, pairing masters of glass with toxicologists, and chocolatiers with pattern specialists. Tony Chambers (1963–), editor-in-chief, says: 'At *Wallpaper** we have very good friends in the design and art worlds and very good friends in the manufacturing world, so we thought it a good idea to bring them together in previously unattempted configurations. Each year we invite, encourage and commission a series of creative cuddles, then sit back and watch wonderful things unfold. It takes interesting and unlikely pairings to produce remarkable and unlikely things.'

By acting as client, patron and creative director, the magazine has helped to establish a recognized platform for innovative partnerships. In a similar way, the Wellcome Collection regularly champions the merging of art and natural sciences. Set up in 2007 as 'the free destination for the incurably curious', the London-based museum proves that existing ideas are even better when they are challenged and seen within new contexts.

The simple step-and-repeat repetition of rhombille tiling is an example of traditional pattern design at the touch of a button.

Bompas & Parr's jelly PATTERN POWER — Superstripe sculptures exemplify the blurring of boundaries and the creativity of collaboration.

The rise in the number of collaborations within the creative industries is also indicative of a wider-reaching craving to reconnect with the physical world. We live in an age where tasks that were once time-consuming can now be easily completed with 'shortcuts' or 'step-and-repeat' commands, in a world where the complex geometries of the Penrose Triangle or Chinese tumbling blocks can be endlessly replicated at the touch of a button. With this technology at our fingertips, we are able to work more instantly and efficiently – yet also more *absently*. With the rise of software such as Adobe's Photoshop, Illustrator and InDesign, and Apple's Final Cut Pro, we are the first creative generation that can hide ourselves away, working behind the private glare of an illuminated device. The digital screen has flattened our daily association with the three-dimensionality of art and design.

Furthermore, we are deluged by information and paralysed by choice; our attention spans have been halved and our desire for instant gratification has more than doubled. Millions of us go about our daily lives staring into a screen; for many it is the first and last thing they look at each and every day. Our brains are entangled in a web of information that is barely tethered to any sort of physical reality. In addition, the proliferation of file sharing and live streaming means that the myriad films we watch and images we see are no longer perceived as physical objects. Take, for example, the ephemeral installations by French artist and photographer Georges Rousse (1947–), in which he transforms abandoned or derelict buildings into pictorial spaces and creates one-of-a-kind artworks that exist only in his photographs. Here, the physical space refracts what we understand from the digital. Rousse's graphic installations make us think about our position as both observer and participant.

LOSING TOUCH | RECONNECTING WITH THE SENSES

The German philosopher Karl Marx (1818–83) suggested that the Industrial Revolution of the late 18th to early 19th century brought about the destruction of the relationship between craftspeople and the goods they produced. As heavy machinery powered by coal, water and steam replaced hand-production methods, creators and consumers lost a deeply rooted human connection with the products and processes of everyday life. Likewise, in the vast and lightning-fast digital era, we are in danger of forgetting a vital connection with the very senses that remind us that we are alive.

However, all is not quite lost and today we can find increasingly innovative inventors collaborating on projects that fight to retain an awareness of the sensory. In 2009, for example, the contemporary food designers and jellymongers Bompas & Parr (Sam Bompas, 1983–, and Harry Parr, 1982–) created the UK's first 'walk-in' cocktail by filling their pop-up bar with a fog of vaporized gin and tonic. They used science and technology to create an immersive, habitable atmosphere, to the delight of all who sampled it. It would seem that the digital screen in front of our faces has, in fact, heightened a synaesthetic desire to see, taste, smell and touch the unseen. Speaking of experiential group dining experiences, Sam Bompas states: 'Digital experiences are all well and good but if you really want to grab someone's attention you need to appeal to the animal within. Sensory and sensual experiences can directly stimulate the beast within all of us. There's a satisfaction there that no screen can ever touch.'

PROBE PROCESSES

CURTAIL CONSUMPTION

In a world of abundance we are often oblivious to the ways in which things are made. From everyday household objects to the food on our plates, we have become disconnected from the manufacturing process. The more we become aware of the world around us, the more we need to start asking questions about where things come from. Who has been affected by our daily wants and requirements? The more we do this, the less we might find ourselves wanting.

Top left, Shipping Shapes, Freight Harbour, Hong Kong | Top right, Crossed Contrails, Switzerland | Bottom left, Road Rainbow, London Bottom right, Scattered Signals, Tel Aviv, Israel

MAKE SENSE

MARVEL AT MATERIALS

As sensory beings in an increasingly digital world, we have lost touch with the materials and textures that make up our environment. Where we have gained speed, efficiency and economic growth, we have lost a vital connection with considered craftsmanship and quality materials. Remembering touch, smell, taste and sound, in addition to the visual, can reconnect us with some of the fundamental and enduring aspects of what it means to be human.

Top left, Tile Pile, Lake District, England | Top right, Breaking Bark, Melbourne | Bottom left, Billow Bulge, Goa, India | Bottom right, Ice Crumble, New York

Our giant PATTERNITY KALEIDOHOME installation celebrates the importance of interaction and play through design.

Salt scattered on plates subjected to varying sound frequencies creates stunning patterns.

This craving for texture, smell and taste has also lead to teamwork of the more corporeal kind. Take, for example, the work created by LucyAndBart (Lucy McRae, 1979–, and Bart Hess, 1984–), who have dedicated their practice to the intensification of fashion, architecture, performance and the body. They are 'body architects', discovering lo-tech prosthetic means for physical enhancement and inventing structures that reshape the human silhouette. Their experiments bring a firm physical reality to a pumped-up, CGI sci-fi aesthetic; and in our digital age, sensing a tactile reality in the apparently superhuman is incredibly invigorating and engaging.

Likewise, PATTERNITY insists that the creative world emerges from its hiding place to work on projects that involve people in multiple and meaningful ways. This is fundamental to all our endeavours, but a recent collaboration with the accommodation website Airbnb, as part of 2014's London Design Festival, explored the idea particularly well. We were commissioned to create a giant installation in the heart of London's Trafalgar Square, and it was crucial to us that we presented something that would inspire hands-on interaction and play, rather than something to merely observe. The result was a 4m- (13ft-) long kaleidoscope that the public could use to place themselves in the centre of their own individual pattern. The 'KALEIDOHOME' (*left*) played with light, texture, sound and the latest in interactive photographic technology that documented real-time interactions with the installation, creating a giant kaleidoscope of imagery online. The aim was to create a unique and joyful experience for those who engaged with it.

BLURRING BOUNDARIES | THE SUM OF PARTS

An additional benefit of collaboration is an introduction to areas that are completely new to us, and working within or adapting to them strengthens our creative and cultural value systems. Working together involves co-operation and finding harmony: good balance within a project requires compromise and the consideration of all ideas. Like all relationships, collaboration fundamentally taps into the human desire to be connected and work together towards a common goal. Take, for example, the partnership between Icelandic singer–songwriter Björk (1965–) and the film-makers Nick Fenton and Peter Strickland in creating the concert film *Biophilia Live* (2014). The film captured the human element of Björk's multidisciplinary, multimedia project *Biophilia*, in which she worked with a wide range of scientists, naturalists and performance artists. One such collaborator was Evan Grant, a creative technologist who specializes in cymatics (the visual representation of sound). Recorded live at London's Alexandra Palace in 2013, *Biophilia Live* featured Björk and her band performing songs using a broad variety of instruments – some digital, some traditional and some completely unclassifiable. The documentary about the making of the show saw the performer in conversation with broadcaster and naturalist David Attenborough, musing on the similarities between the properties of minerals in the natural world and the sounds and rhythmic patterns of her music. It is a perfect example of how the act of exploring a specialism through a new lens can lead to new ideas of vital originality.

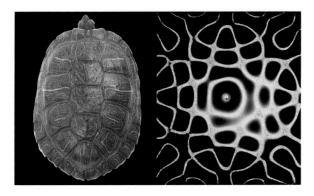

From a shell to a song, we are all linked by invisible commonalities that we are only just beginning to understand.

With the whole world flattened behind our screens, we are increasingly seeking hands-on experiences and authentic connectivity.

The components of an everyday toaster as laid out in Thomas Thwaites' *The Toaster Project*.

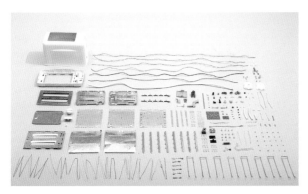

'We are like islands in the sea, separate on the surface but connected in the deep.'
William James (1842 —1910), American philosopher and psychologist

A RUDE AWAKENING | CONSCIOUS CONSUMPTION

Our world of material abundance has left us increasingly disconnected from the many processes that even a humdrum table lamp has gone through before we plug it in. We are so used to 'off the peg' and 'ready-made' that even making a chip from a potato can seem demanding, let alone fathoming how a microchip comes into being. We know so little about the things we spend most of our lives with, and this becomes increasingly problematic as we come to be more and more reliant upon them. There is undoubtedly a creative desire to re-engage with material and form, and we are increasingly drawn towards more traditional and considered ways of making. In an age of conspicuous consumption, there is considerable comfort to be taken from craftsmanship that is produced using carefully devised methods and techniques.

The 2011 non-narrative documentary film *Samsara*, directed by Ron Fricke, explores the wonders and horrors of our world, from the mundane to the mass-manufactured, in astounding detail. In a non-verbal, almost trance-like fashion, *Samsara* takes us on a visual and emotional journey from the natural to the man-made, the spiritual to the superfluous. With visuals reminiscent of Andreas Gursky's large-format photography of factory lines and supermarket aisles, *Samsara* – part documentary, part travelogue, part guided meditation – allows us to sit back and see with fresh eyes what it means, for good and for bad, to be in the world today.

In such a world, where so much of the infrastructure upon which we have become reliant is out of sight and far from our minds and conscience, we have a renewed desire to understand how things have been created. Documentary series such as the Discovery Channel's *How It's Made* (first aired in January 2001) feed this curiosity. Whether it's focusing on a handcrafted glass marble, going through a careful process of dipping, rolling and melting, or the manufacture of solar panels, the series provides bite-sized explorations into how things actually come into being. And in an increasingly overloaded world, there's a rising moral obligation for us all to fully understand the ways in which things have been made.

This very theme was also explored in 'In The Making', a travelling exhibition organized by London's Design Museum in 2014. Curated by award-winning British designers Edward Barber (1969–) and Jay Osgerby (1969–), the show presented 24 objects, from a tennis ball to a trumpet, in states of mid-manufacture. By exhibiting such objects in an incomplete state, the magnificence of the manufacturing process came to life. At the same time the museum also displayed 'Hello, My Name is Paul Smith', an exhibition that presented the work and career of the esteemed British fashion designer Paul Smith (1946–), with a similar 'bringing to life' at the core of the show. Through the use of film and installation, visitors were able to wander through a re-creation of his design studio, where garment patterns hung above sewing machines and spools of wool. The exhibition threw a spotlight on both the complicated processes and the many specialist hands involved in creating the resulting runway pieces.

Katie Gaudion's co-designed textile toys use
materials to help engage and explore.

Nepalese Fair Trade workers in the process of
crafting a rug of our own design.

Another designer exploring the intricacies of production and illuminating just how things are made is Thomas Thwaites, who initiated *The Toaster Project* (see image at the bottom of page 117) in 2010. The project had a simple aim: to build a domestic toaster from scratch, beginning by mining the raw minerals to make metal and extracting plastic from oil. Thwaites's book, *The Toaster Project: Or a Heroic Attempt to Build a Simple Electric Appliance from Scratch* (2011), provides a rude awakening as to what really goes into an anonymous kitchen appliance. This return to understanding the processes behind the things we use every day provides the perfect platform to observe the world through fresh eyes.

> *'In all affairs it's a healthy thing now and then to hang a question mark on the things you have long taken for granted.'*
> Bertrand Russell (1872–1970), British philosopher and mathematician

PATTERNITY welcomes and celebrates this new era of convergence: a time where specialists can join together and explore new ideas in other formats. It is vital that those from science join with the arts and vice versa. For example, ideas traditionally linked with scientific fields are thoughtfully explored in the 'Occupational Textiles' made by designer Katie Gaudion (1979–). The name is in homage to educationalists Friedrich Froebel (1782–1852) and Maria Montessori (1870–1952), and the field of occupational therapy. Gaudion holds a Master of Philosophy in Textile Design from the Royal College of Art and her specialist interest lies in co-designing with adults and children with learning disabilities and neurological conditions. She developed a range of gender-neutral textile toys for all ages, including 'Springy Thingy' (above left), which stimulate the primary senses of touch, sound, smell and sight as well as encouraging movement and play for those with sensory processing dysfunctions. Each toy explores the somatic nature of textiles with the aim of accentuating the sensory experience.

VENTURING BENEATH THE SURFACE | VISUALIZING THE UNSEEN

By 2011 the specialist pattern research we had amassed online was really only the tip of the iceberg of our activities. The PATTERNITY server was overflowing, and had become in itself a fertile breeding ground for new project ideas and future collaborations. Hailed by the creative industry as the 'go-to authority' on pattern, it wasn't long before we were approached to work on our first collaboration. The publisher Granta invited us to work on our first pattern-focused PATTERNITY STUDIO project: a cover illustration for E C Osondu's *Voice of America*. Our brief was to depict and simplify the content of the book (stories of Nigeria and America and the bonds that connect the two) into a visual pattern, and we set about designing a graphic that served to illustrate what lay beneath the surface. It was a simple idea that underscored the PATTERNITY approach of using pattern as a narrative tool to visualize the unseen – in this case the behavioural patterns of two nations. The opportunity of using our research in collaboration with another specialist was an exciting and appealing development.

Our Phase Bureau brought traditional marquetry craft together with a contemporary aesthetic.

William Morris played a significant role in the British textile and craft industries as well as the wider socialist movement. Morris took much inspiration from nature, as shown by his Acanthus tapestry, created in 1874.

Within months a diverse range of projects had been proposed to us and soon the fully-fledged PATTERNITY STUDIO was working on a range of special projects and collaborations. Our backgrounds as art director and surface designer meant that we had the balance of skills to set up a consultancy studio organized to work on concept-led projects that meet our values and longer-term ambitions for PATTERNITY. Our approach, which is far-reaching yet focused, uses in-depth research and the innovative implementation of pattern with an aim to push the expectations of traditional surface design. Working on all aspects of design and art direction, from print and packaging to film-making, photography and 3-D installation, our award-winning design collaborations and commissions use pattern to delve beneath the surface and help to bring our in-depth and ongoing research of pattern to life.

'No pattern should be without some sort of meaning.'
William Morris (1834–1896), textile designer, socialist and father of the Arts and Crafts Movement

NEW DISCOVERIES | THE SEARCH FOR MEANING

Partnership has the power to traverse eras, disciplines and fields, breathing new life and interest into materials and processes that invariably lead to new discoveries. The breaking down of established patterns challenges and invigorates our everyday landscape. Modern technology combined with traditional materials can also yield timeless results. Through the implementation of our exhaustive research, our patterns tell worthwhile stories about the world in which we live. They manifest as unique outcomes, drawing attention, merging boundaries and driving forward innovation.

We explored this with one of our first PATTERNITY projects – a furniture collaboration with marquetry specialist Toby Winteringham. Launched in 2010, the collection used bold, colourful, geometric patterns rarely seen in traditional marquetry (an ancient Chinese craft dating back to *c.*2600BC, more commonly associated with delicate natural shapes such as leaves and flowers). Our pattern application projects begin as a conversation with the collaborator about a product or craft's history and technique – in this case the skill and materials involved in marquetry, which became prominent in the 16th century. We began the method of applying pieces of veneer together to form decorative patterns, inspired by fleeting shadows cast on scaffolding in everyday urban environments. The resulting piece, entitled 'Shift', referenced the shifting of light, the passing of time, acceptance and change. It was fitting that 'Shift' went on to win us our first *Wallpaper** Design Award for our innovative approach to an under-appreciated technique. The most rewarding aspect of the project was that the application of pattern had brought a new lease of life to Winteringham's traditional practice. The collaboration showcased the power of deeply considered pattern to reinvigorate and add new meaning.

In a world of transitory trends that come and go (and then reappear at an alarming rate), the concept and the craft have become disconnected in mass production, adding stresses to the often strained relationship between surface decoration and the concept of 'good' design. Can, for example, the application of surface pattern

119

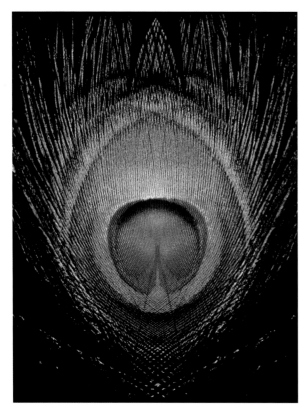

A peacock feather reminds us of the power pattern has to decorate and draw attention.

Our project with The Environmental Justice Foundation used pattern to visualize vital conservational data.

on everything from refrigerators to flooring be anything other than a way of camouflaging substandard workmanship? The discussion of decoration relative to purpose was a key argument in 20th-century thought. The Austrian-Czech architect Adolf Loos (1870–1933) made a powerful denunciation of unnecessary ornamentation in a lecture given in 1910 (later published as *Ornament and Crime*). The baton was later taken up by Charles-Édouard Jeanneret-Gris (better known as the pioneer of modern architecture, Le Corbusier, 1887–1965) in a series of articles entitled 'Decorative Art of Today' in his magazine *L'Esprit Nouveau*. First published in 1925, Le Corbusier was writing in protest about the prevalence of the decorative, decadent Art Deco style that proliferated at the 'Exposition Internationale des Arts Décoratifs et Industriels Modernes' that same year.

'Trash', he wrote, 'is always abundantly decorated; the luxury object is well made, neat and clean, pure and healthy, and its bareness reveals the quality of its manufacture … Decorative is disguise.' The contemporary vogue for decorating anything and everything was, in his view, 'a false taste, an abominable little perversion'. Yet, despite this polemic, Le Corbusier clearly exhibited a profound interest in system and pattern within his proposals for urban planning. As can be seen, the architect's vision, dedicated to 'providing better living conditions for the residents of crowded cities', was of a new modern city in which identical towers set on fixed, linear grids shoot up into the air in a regular, repetitive pattern.

On the other hand, the mathematician and philosopher Alfred North Whitehead (1861–1947) noted that we derive 'significant aesthetic enjoyment' from pattern and ought to reconsider the humanness of such decoration – we are pattern-seeking creatures after all. There is a fundamental joy connected with pattern recognition that should not be undervalued. Joy and the search for meaning, both being fundamental driving aspects of humanity, should come into the conversation.

'Design, stripped to its essence, can be defined as the human capacity to shape and make our environment in ways without precedent in nature, to serve our needs and give meaning to our lives.'
Professor John Heskett (1937–2014), academic and author

NARRATIVE DESIGN | TELLING WORTHWHILE STORIES

To deal with the overwhelming cacophony of one-dimensional surface ornamentation spread over arbitrary objects all around us, it is vital to delve beneath the surface. We must consider what the more social and psychological implications of patterns are and, more importantly, how we can learn from pattern to positively shape the world around us.

A lot of our working process at PATTERNITY revolves around collaborating with brands and crafts that we feel have a valuable story to tell – a story that can be told through the use of pattern. We actively seek projects that enable us to merge our pattern innovation with iconic products and specialist crafts. The ethical knitwear collection we designed with British label Chinti and Parker (see pages 96–7), for example, used

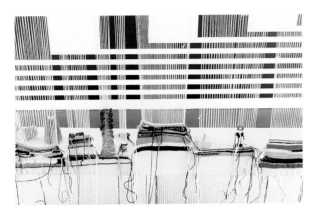

An interactive weaving collaboration with textiles pioneer Katherine May aimed to foster socialization through proximity, at the PATTERN POWER — Superstripe festival in 2013.

A herd-like migration to meaningful projects and collaborations will pave the way towards a positive and sustainable future.

pattern to encourage a more conscious awareness of the world and its buying habits. The 'Fleet of Dazzle' project with London's Imperial War Museums (see pages 56–7) allowed us to use pattern in order to share the stories of war and the importance of unity at a time of increasing conflict. The range of teaware that we worked on with designer Richard Brendon (see pages 136–7) used pattern to tell a story of social mobility, a mobility that was encouraged, in part, thanks to the arrival of tea as a replacement for alcohol among the aristocracy in 17th-century England. Although abstract, we fused a coded message with a traditional craft; all of the ceramics were made by artisans in Stoke-on-Trent, the home of British pottery. The application of pattern to a product has to add value, a value loaded with meaning and authenticity.

In blurring boundaries between disciplines we have collaborated and consulted with individuals, specialists and institutions across the worlds of fashion and interiors, art and architecture, food and drink, science and technology, and education. Diverse projects are unified by their use of the power of pattern to tell worthwhile stories about the world. One of these special projects was our collaboration with the Environmental Justice Foundation (pictured opposite below), which used pattern to visualize data and raise awareness of the damaging effects of bottom trawling on the world's seabeds – a pattern that had purpose both on and beneath the surface.

At PATTERNITY, we never implement a pattern without first asking several key questions – can this pattern tell us something interesting or important about the world in which we live? Does this pattern encourage a more positive connection to the world around us? Will this pattern draw attention to the bigger picture?

REDEFINING CREATIVITY | A COLLABORATIVE CULTURE

In a world dominated by commercial and capitalist icons, where global brands are symbols for success and power, we must allow specialists to explore areas that they have never experienced before in order to make new and important discoveries. It will allow us to fundamentally shift the commonly held perception of what it means to be 'creative'. The act of being creative should not be limited to the worlds of art and design. We all have the ability to create, and central to creativity is the way we see the world, finding inspiration and opportunities in unexpected and often ignored places. It is embedded in a desire to challenge and engage perception. Often the only way to create something pioneering is to be able to step back and see it afresh. In a more competitive creative world, we should be working together, forging new and authentic opportunities and relationships. These opportunities are endless when we choose to think and work outside of what we already know and understand. As ex-advertising executive and cultural commentator Mark Earls (1961–) has said, 'We are innately hardwired to work as a herd; and this way of working can be highly rewarding both creatively and socially – both locally and globally.' There is great value in collaborating and we have much to learn from each other.

'No man is an island entire of itself; every man is a piece of the continent, a part of the main.'
John Donne (1572–1631), English metaphysical poet

A marble in mid-manufacture proves the
magnificence in the making of the mundane.

In many ways, human thought and actions are manifest in tangible products and materials. What we create and consume is guided by what we think both individually and collectively. With this in mind, it would appear that we are living in a time of sharp contrasts: a time where both the mass-produced and the meticulously crafted collide. The rise of collaboration, craftsmanship and co-creation within the creative fields provides an indication that we are moving into an age spirited by new ways of doing. The effects of this change could be wide reaching, as this co-operative approach has the power to move us away from the narrow individualistic mindset of the past, leading us into a time that further embraces the concept of 'we' over 'I'. This has the power to lead us to a more humble and open environment of learning and discovery – a fertile breeding ground for partnerships and future innovation.

As Thomas Kuhn (1922–96), the physicist, historian and philosopher wrote in *The Structure of Scientific Revolutions* (1962): 'The radical breakthroughs tend to come from just three sources: young people, accidents and the cross-fertilization of disciplines.' A harmonious development of the modern world relies on creative and questioning minds, joined together to ask bigger questions, such as: How is this product made? How many hands and by-products have been involved in the making of this material? How far has this item travelled before it reaches my supermarket shelf? These questions are essential in order to reconnect the dots once again. Identifying inefficiencies and inequalities within the existing patterns of thought and action will lead to a worldwide revolution, based on balanced and sustainable ways of co-existing and creating.

'We are born for co-operation'
Marcus Aurelius (AD121—180), philosopher, Roman emperor

Right, Blue Bag Face, Stuart C Wilson,
Isamaya Ffrench for Christopher Shannon.

Carried away by a wave of waste, it is time to
reconsider the way we create and consume.

Pages 126–7, Spiral Rounds, Neil Watson,
design: Katie Gaudion

∞ CONCEPT + CRAFT CONVERGED

●● SUM MARQUETRY TABLE

At PATTERNITY we are committed to understanding the manufacturing processes behind all our products and projects. We are proud to use the power of pattern to add meaning and value – breathing new life into traditional crafts and heritage techniques. The 'Sum Table' (right) is a follow-up collaboration with UK-based traditional marquetry specialist and furniture maker Toby Winteringham. The modular piece was the focus of our debut cultural biennale 'PATTERN POWER – Superstripe', around which multidisciplinary 'PATTERNITALKS' were hosted. These round-table discussions (below) brought together some of the world's leading specialists from art and design, science, health and mathematics, and explored how a shared awareness and understanding of life's patterns can positively shape the world around us. The table's bold monochrome stripes, which converge towards the centre of the circle and split into two halves, represent the sum of many parts coming together; an homage to equality, ideas and the unifying nature of pattern beneath the surface.

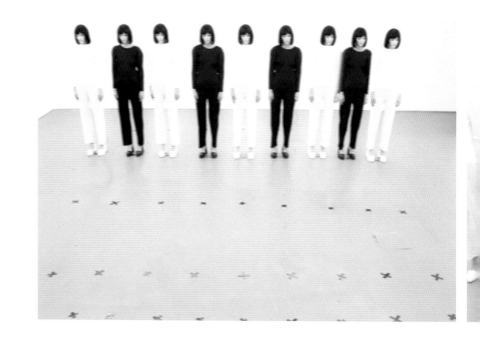

▶ WHEN STRIPES COLLIDE

PATTERN POWER | FILM PROJECT

Commissioned for our cultural festival 'PATTERN POWER – Superstripe', *When Stripes Collide* was a film made in collaboration with Lily Silverton, fashion features editor at *POP* magazine. The film featured the creations of multidisciplinary textile designer Katie Gaudion, whose work with people of all abilities investigates how harnessing the sensory qualities of materials can improve a person's experience of their surroundings. Gaudion and Silverton explored the link between patterns of the mind and environment further at one of a series of round-table 'PATTERNTALKS' for the duration of the month-long festival in Spring 2013.

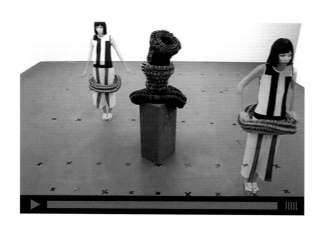

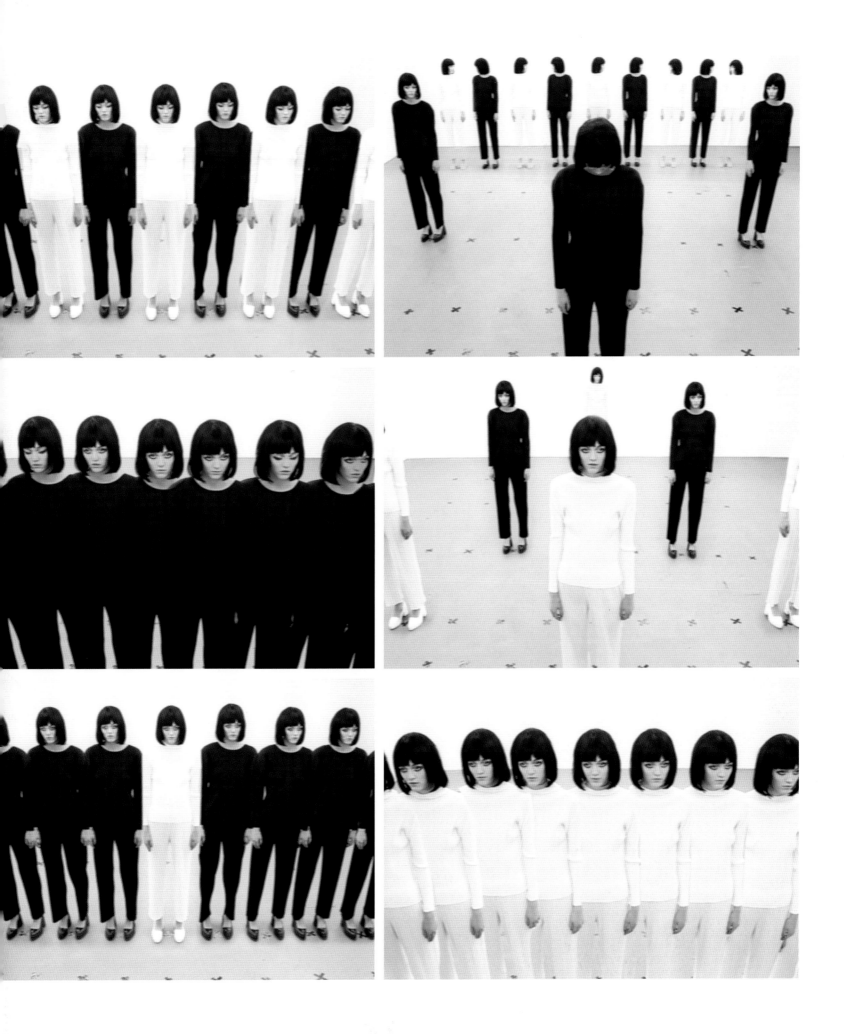

∞ WOVEN WONDERS

FAIR-TRADE RUG COLLECTION

We were approached by non-profit social business Made by Node to collaborate on a special project in association with Kumbeshwar Technical School in Kathmandu. At PATTERNITY we are proud to use the power of pattern to bring attention to wider and worthwhile issues, in this case the importance of fair-trade manufacture. The bold, monochrome rug designs (see page 107 and right) pay homage to traditional Nepalese carpet making and the drying process, which involves finished rugs being draped over the jagged rooftops to dry in the midday sun.

By learning the skill of weaving, artisan employees of Kumbeshwar Technical School are able to earn a wage and their work supports a school of 260 children and an orphanage of 19 (below). A film showing what goes on beneath the surface of our collaboration can be watched at PATTERNITY.ORG.

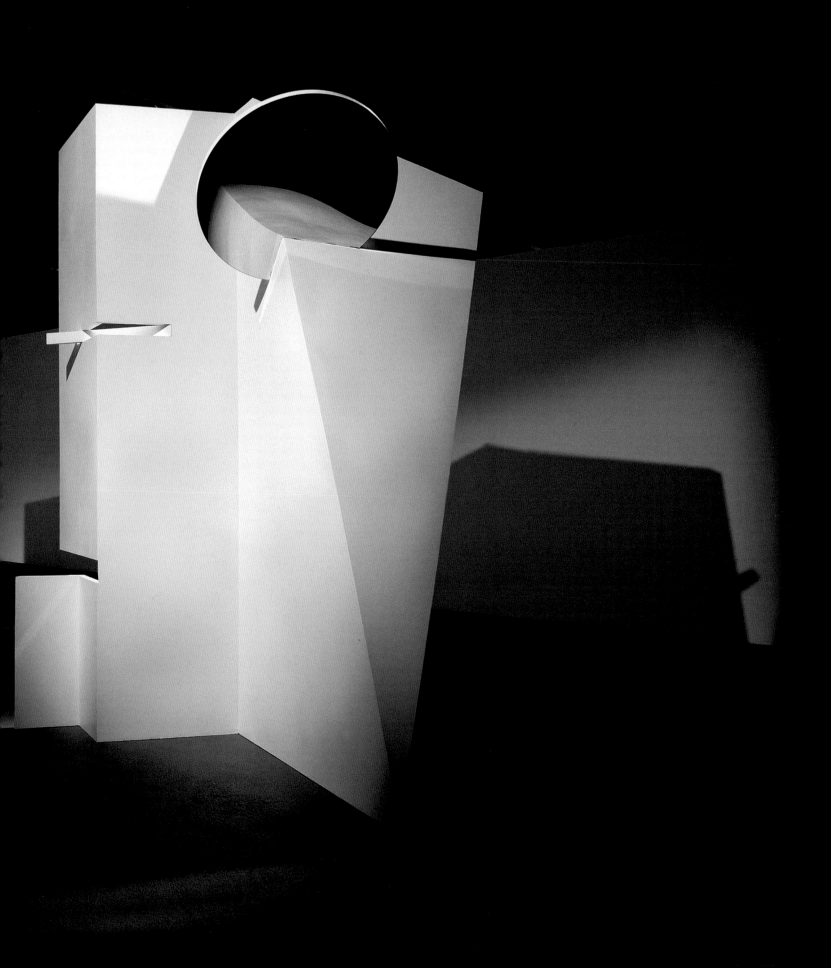

Pages 136—7, Warp + Reason Ceramics,
PATTERNITY ∞ Richard Brendon, cobalt blue,
burnished gold, bone China

◆ THE STRUCTURE OF CHOCOLATE

EDUCATIONAL EDIBLE INSTALLATION

For *Wallpaper** Handmade 2014 we teamed up with Belgian chocolatier Pierre Marcolini and marquetry specialist Toby Winteringham to create a 'Structure of Chocolate' (right). The blueprint of the piece was a single hexagonal molecule of the chocolate compound theobromine (below), with each individual element represented by a pattern and a shape in modular marquetry form. The result was a unique fusion between science, craft and taste, as Pierre Marcolini's chocolate perfectly embellished the marquetry structure both on and beneath the surface, infused with a unique flavour by the wood encasing it. The chocolate display celebrates the unifying nature of pattern – implemented as a powerful tool with which to educate and inspire.

THEOBROMINE

Pages 140—1, PATTERNITY KALEIDOHOME,
Ed Gilligan, Trafalgar Square, London

■ PATTERNS TO TAKE EVERYWHERE

STREETSHAPES HOSIERY

PATTERNITY hosiery began as an extension of our brand philosophy. They are a wearable celebration of the patterns that surround us all wherever we go. We believe it's important that our manifesto extends into products that people can integrate into everyday life. Launched at Selfridges, London, the designs are based on the fundamental shapes that make up all matter – a bold rearrangement of circles, lines, triangles and squares. In our fast-paced world, it's important to be reminded daily that these shapes are an enduring part of life. They have the power to remind us to pay attention and feel part of a much bigger picture. We wanted to create wearable patterns that would represent the PATTERNITY brand values – values synonymous with a positive way of seeing and being.

'All are but parts of one stupendous whole'.

Alexander Pope (1688–1744), English poet

PART THREE

CONNECTIVITY

EXPLORATION | FROM THE MICRO
TO THE MACRO

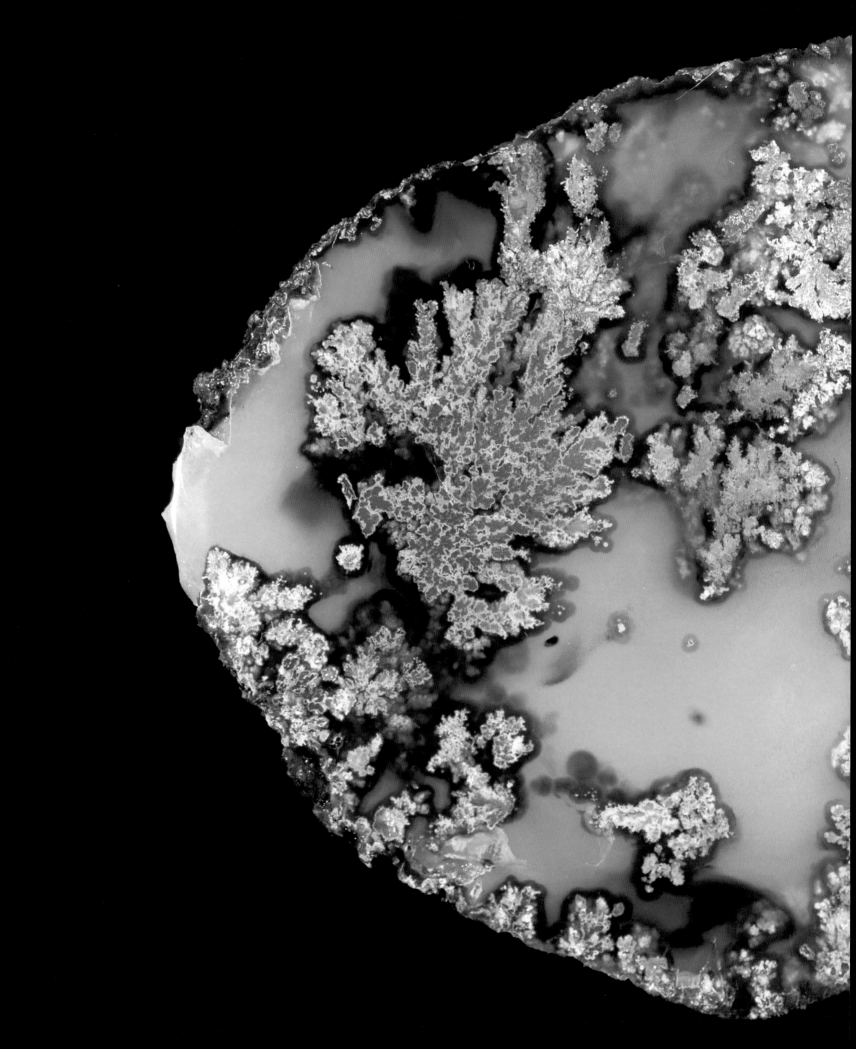

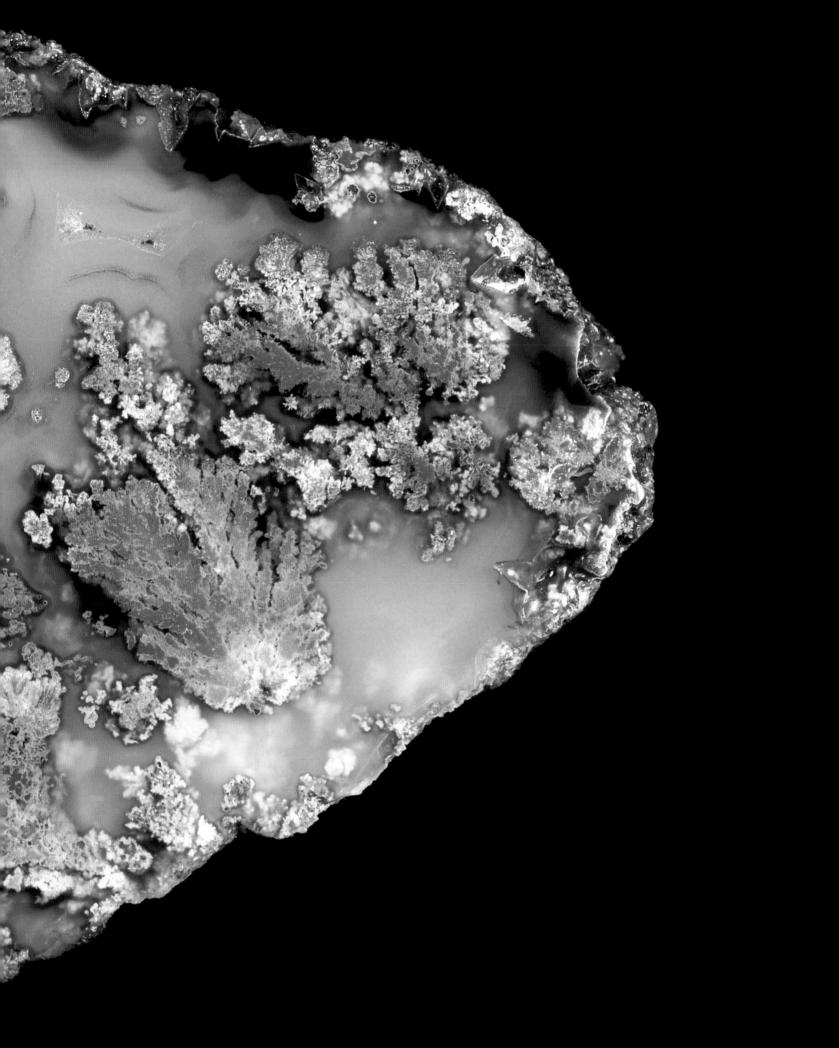

Pages 144–5, Bouquet Agate, D. R. 'Matt' Dillon, Texas, USA

Left, Paint Power, Thomas Brown, set: Lightning + Kinglyface | Right, Floral Flash, Viviane Sassen, fashion: Gucci

'All that is in tune with Thee, O Universe, is in tune with me.'

Marcus Aurelius (AD121–180), philosopher and Roman emperor

Left, Creature Curls, Tim Flach, centipedes | Right, Body Bind, Gamma Rapho, fashion: Iris Van Herpen

'The goal of life is living in agreement with nature.'

Zeno Of Elea (c.490–430BC), Greek philosopher

From aerial images of Earth shot from afar (above) to the Large Hadron Collider — the world's largest particle accelerator — (below), our understanding of our place within the world has been expanded.

THE POWER OF CONNECTIVITY | SHIFTING PERSPECTIVE

To explore is to venture into the unknown. From Christopher Columbus's voyage to the Americas in 1492 to Edmund Hillary's arrival at the summit of Mount Everest in 1953, names of legendary pioneers are marked on the timeline of human discovery, and their efforts across land and sea have provided us with a compass with which to navigate our own environments.

Explorers systematically and strategically examine their surroundings, pushing us towards a more common goal of collective discovery. This seeking out of new opportunities and ways of thinking for the benefit of the greater good is at the heart of everything we do at PATTERNITY.

Exploration gives us a new and more expansive sense of home. Not only are we living in a time where we can travel further than ever before, thanks to low-cost travel and the sprawling web of information that is the internet, but we also live on a planet where discoveries on both macro and micro scales are continually being made. In August 2012 the unmanned probe *Voyager 1* (first launched in 1977) became the first human-made object to enter the unexplored region between stars known as 'interstellar space'. It has travelled further than anything or anyone in human history. The following year the Large Hadron Collider – built at CERN (the European Organisation for Nuclear Research), near Geneva, in collaboration with over 10,000 scientists and engineers from over 100 countries – confirmed the identification of the smallest particle known to man.

> *'Where the telescope ends, the microscope begins.*
> *Which of the two has the grander view?'*
> Victor Hugo (1802–85), poet, novelist and dramatist

This sense of living somewhere between these startling and inconceivable scales was explored in a short documentary film written and directed by American designers Charles and Ray Eames. *Powers of Ten* (1977) depicts the relative size of things in the universe, beginning with a couple having a picnic, but quickly expanding from the park in which they are sitting to the whole city, to the entire planet – expanding outwards in distances increasing by the power of ten until the known universe is dramatically surveyed. The film then pauses and makes the return voyage inwards, zooming back to the couple and into the human body to a point where a single atom and its elementary particles can be observed. Made long before the days of Google Earth, the film allows the viewer to momentarily step back and gain a sense of awe at the very essence of human existence. The patterns deep within us as cells and DNA are miraculously mirrored in the patterns of the cosmos as we know it. Watching *Powers of Ten*, you feel both microscopically insignificant and almighty. We are connected beyond comprehension, biologically, chemically and atomically, to our environment and everything in it.

> *'There is no man alone, because every man is a microcosm,*
> *and carries the whole world about him.'*
> Sir Thomas Browne (1605-1682), English polymath and author

From trees to lungs, the patterns deep within us are also the patterns far beyond us.

From craniums (below left) to cabbages (below right), focusing on our internal connectivity to nature opens new doors to our collective consciousness.

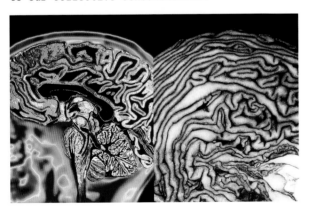

A UNIVERSAL LANGUAGE | STEPPING BACK

Today the opportunities to explore are relatively egalitarian. What lies far away in the ether is fuel for our endless curiosity. What lies beneath has the force to drive forward future innovation, springing forth inferences, theories and human understanding. But now that humanity has virtually conquered every last corner of the world, it feels timely that a new approach be established, allowing us collectively to stand back, pause and observe. This is an approach that goes back to basics, picking up some of the most fundamental laws and languages of the inner workings of nature. As Sufi musician and guide Hazrat Inayat Khan (1882–1927) described it, 'Living in the world without insight into the hidden laws of nature is like not knowing the language of the country in which one was born.' This is a form of exploration that takes a more holistic and humble approach; a stance so obvious that it could be as simple as a walk in the park.

When taking a stroll through a rural landscape our eyes are drawn to numerous patterns, from the texture of tree bark to the astounding symmetry of sunflower seeds or the spiral structure of a pinecone. Looking around, you might imagine that branches and their leaves are arranged at random, potentially generated in a haphazard manner, perhaps not dissimilar to the Abstract Expressionist 'drip' paintings of Jackson Pollock (1912–56). However, just as Pollock carefully orchestrated his trickles of paint, the arrangement of even the most common tree owes more to pattern than you might think. These observations might seem chaotic or random at first, but there are no accidents in nature and all these phenomena have an innate logic; there is a pattern within the points at which every branch, leaf, stem, bud or seed emerges. There is wisdom at work.

Despite the astonishing variety of seemingly disconnected formations within the natural world – from swirling river deltas to the delicate veins in a leaf, and from the bronchi of our lungs to the branches high above our heads – many have closely comparable, sometimes indistinguishable features when viewed under the microscope or from a satellite. For example, you can break off a tiny floret from a white cauliflower and observe that it resembles a minute version of the previous whole. These patterns high above, down below and deep within us are evidence of nature's miraculous dance to which, while it can't always be technically described, we are all somehow inherently connected. These striking similarities could be considered to be some form of ancient, universal language – one that we are only just beginning to rediscover.

'There is not a fragment in all nature, for every relative fragment of one thing is a full harmonious unit in itself.'
John Muir (1838–1914), Scottish-American
naturalist and author

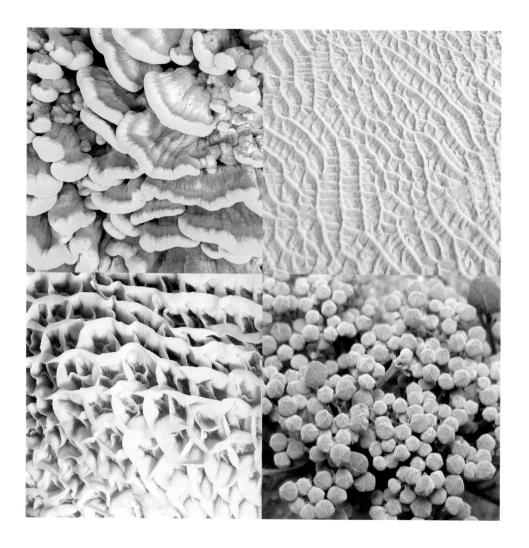

LOOK CLOSER

MUSE ON THE MICRO

Contemplating what might be on the end of your fork or growing in your garden can have small but resonant results. Looking closely at the veins of a leaf or the cracks in the pavement can help to uncover some of the intrinsic truisms of life. Careful consideration of nature's most fundamental formations has lead mankind to some of its most powerful discoveries – nature really is the most efficient engineer.

Top left, Fungus Fans, Carmel Beach, California | Top right, Sand Contours, Norfolk, England | Bottom left, Tripe Ripples, sheep offal Bottom right, Pollen Pops, Botanical Gardens, Rio De Janeiro, Brazil

STEP BACK

MARVEL AT THE MACRO

We are so often absorbed by the necessities of modern life that we forget to look up and remember the awe-inspiring capacity of the great beyond. Realizing that we constitute a tiny fragment of a much bigger, universal picture has the power to bring perspective to our daily disputes and disappointments. It is important to rediscover the wonder that humanity once felt when looking up at the stars.

Top left, Lichen Landscape, Ilha Grande, Brazil | Top right, Arid and Aerial, Arizona, USA | Bottom left, Woven Layers, Bogotá, Columbia Bottom right, Tangled Treads, Lanzarote

The spiralling head of Romanesco broccoli has the power to project the viewer into a calm and meditative state.

As mentioned in Part One, this 'universal language' of similarity was popularized by the mathematician Benoît Mandelbrot, who dedicated much of his life to digging beneath the surface of the irregular patterns of the natural world. Mandelbrot observed that there was a pattern in certain aspects of nature that could not be accurately described in existing mathematical terms. In the 1960s he began to study the geometry of a wide variety of irregular natural phenomena and realized that many of these forms were composed by successive subdivisions – that is to say 'repeating patterns', of simple polygons or polyhedra, described by Mandelbrot as 'fractals'. In what came to be known as 'fractal geometry', the mathematician created a system to describe and analyse the complexity of the irregular shapes in nature. His pioneering studies into these naturally repeating phenomena allow us to grasp the complexity of pattern within shapes that are grainy, tangled, wispy or wrinkled.

Mandelbrot represented his discoveries through mathematical equations and then used early IBM software to plot these numbers, resulting in complex and mesmerizing fractal computer graphics. Mandelbrot found that things typically considered chaotic – such as clouds or shorelines – actually had a 'degree of order'. This powerful discovery said much about the current understanding of the universe and indeed our place within it. Mandelbrot's 'language to speak of clouds' had been written.

CELEBRATING COINCIDENCE | CURIOUS COMMONALITIES

An internet search for 'Mandelbrot' today brings up a fascinating array of forums, videos and blogs associated with LSD and psychedelia, with countless reports of similar visual phenomena to Mandelbrot's fractal imagery being experienced by many when under the influence of hallucinogenic stimulants. It is interesting to observe that Mandelbrot's discoveries have been wholly embraced not only by his peers within scientific and mathematic fields, but also by disparate, countercultural and, in some cases, renegade communities. These curious commonalities between seemingly segregated areas, remind us, like Mandelbrot's findings themselves, of our small part in a much greater tapestry, much of which is yet to be fully understood.

The hexagonal rock formations at Giant's Causeway, Ireland, remind us of nature's expert architectural engineering.

'No coincidence, no story.'
Chinese proverb

We could go so far as to say that the patterns and coincidences within the natural world are signposts that urge us towards future innovation. It is exciting to imagine that inspiration for the next biological breakthrough could come after a simple trip to buy groceries. Looking, for instance, at the bright green, spiral shape of Romanesco broccoli, it is natural to wonder what kind of creative genius would have the patience to concoct such a magnificent form. Even a casual observer would be mesmerized by its spontaneous architectural domes and perfect repetition. Like staring up at the night's sky, delving into the world of naturally occurring patterns can have humbling and deeply resonating results, sparking philosophical ruminations on life and the universe. As the English naturalist Sir Joseph Banks (1743–1820) wrote in 1772, on

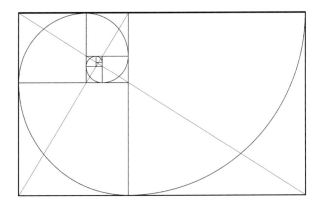

A diagram illustrating the recursive mathematical spiralling of the golden ratio.

The principles of the golden ratio can be found in many natural forms from ancient Ammonite fossils (below), to the latest images from NASA's Hubble Space Telescope of the Whirlpool Galaxy (bottom).

observing the naturally prismatic geometric rock formations of Fingal's Cave on the Scottish island of Staffa: 'Compared to this what are the cathedrals and palaces built by men! Mere models or playthings, imitations as diminutive as his works will always be when compared with those of nature.'

But how can we begin to make sense of the many patterns that shape the world around us? How many patterns are there? When you take into account variations of colour, repetition and scale there are thousands – especially in the man-made world. However, when it comes to nature's palette their manifestations are reassuringly few. As science writer and pattern specialist Philip Ball (1962–) describes it: 'Many patterns in nature have a universal aspect that does not respect the traditional divisions between the natural sciences, or even between the living and the non-living world.' Even in systems that appear to have nothing in common, the same patterns manifest. There is comfort and familiarity to be found in the self-regulating systems of the natural world and, with the right attention, we have much to learn from them.

'All things are full of signs, and it is a wise man who can learn about one thing from another.'
Plotinus (AD205–270), Roman Neo-Platonist philosopher

Despite this apparent simplicity, understanding the patterns that shape the universe feels like a supremely daunting task. In order to begin to dig beneath the surface, we must make a geometrical expedition to 13th-century Italy and the desk and mind of mathematician Leonardo of Pisa, known as Fibonacci (*c*.1170–1250). Fibonacci brought a new and enthusiastic audience to the wonders of mathematics with his weighty, handwritten, 600-page book, *Liber Abaci* ('Book of Calculation', 1202) and a deceptively simple list of numbers. Fibonacci travelled far and wide to study with Arab mathematicians, and he returned with a numbered sequence in which each number is made by adding the previous two together – 0 1 1 2 3 5 8 13 21 – in a pattern that continues infinitely and is now known as the Fibonacci sequence.

The sequence is just as relevant today as it was in 1202. Look at most plants – whether tomato, strawberry or pineapple, count the number of petals, or the way the leaves are arranged, and you will find them set out in pairs, threes, fives, eights or thirteens. You will recognize these numbers in the five-seed chambers of an apple, or the 34 or 55 spiral whorls in a sunflower head. This simple recursive pattern occurs so frequently in nature that it is a challenge to find a plant or fruit structure that does not conform. There is even music in the mathematics. Although popularized by Fibonacci, this sequence of recursive growth originally dates back to 1200BC in ancient India, where it was used as a method of counting rhythm. This is an example of yet more curious coincidences that mirror other aspects of life as we know it; there are patterns within the patterns that extend like threads far back in time and space.

'Invisible threads are the strongest ties.'
Friedrich Nietzsche (1844–1900), philologist,
philosopher, cultural critic and poet

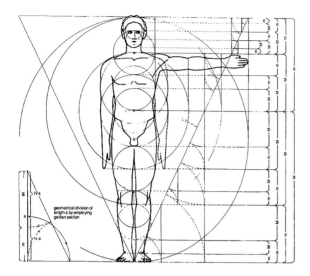

This illustration showing how the human figure relates to the golden ratio was published in architect Ernst Neufert's book *Architect's Data* (1936) about ergonomics and the spatial requirements of buildings.

A still taken from Benjamin Seroussi's film *Divine Proportions* (2012), which explores the link between perceptions of beauty and mathematics.

JOURNEYING INTO GEOMETRY | DIVINE PROPORTIONS

Venturing forth, as these ratios of consecutive numbers get progressively closer to a single number (1.618034 to the first six decimal places), it would be impossible not to examine the curious Golden Ratio – a number so embedded into the fabric of the universe that it has inspired and haunted humanity for thousands of years. Also known as the 'divine section', the Golden Ratio has long been considered to have almost mystical properties, even so far as being represented in our bodily proportions. In fact, it is fair to say that the Golden Ratio has inspired thinkers of all disciplines like no other number in the history of mathematics.

The figure is supposed to represent the 'ideal' proportion, one that has regularly been used as a basis for countless creative and constructive outcomes. From the classical architecture of the Parthenon to the 20th-century works of architect Le Corbusier and artist Salvador Dalí, countless numbers have proportioned their works to approximate the Golden Ratio. The ratio has also been used to analyse the proportions of natural objects, such as the flowering of an artichoke or the uncurling of a fern, as well as other biological sequences, such as the family trees of honeybees. As we become more aware of these spontaneous formations in the natural world, from the minute to the gigantic, we begin to consider the wider picture. A new kind of greater creative force is called into question.

> *'Pattern formation is a fundamental property of physical laws*
> *– a kind of spontaneous creativity in the universe.'*
> Philip Ball (1962–), science writer

Some of the greatest mathematical minds have spent endless hours pondering the Golden Ratio and its 'mystical' properties. As the German mathematician, astronomer and astrologer Johannes Kepler (1571–1630) said: 'Where there is matter, there is geometry'. But this fascination is not confined purely to calculus. Over the centuries biologists, artists, musicians, historians, architects, psychologists and even mystics have reflected on and debated the basis of the ratio's appeal and ubiquity in the natural world. More recently, the Paris-based film-maker Benjamin Seroussi (1980–) was commissioned by web-based film channel NOWNESS to make *Divine Proportions* (2012), a moving scientific exploration of the body, which unpacks the mysterious qualities of the Golden Ratio associated with our conception of beauty and bodily proportion through a modern lens. Our innate curiosity is taking on new shapes and forms.

Venturing onwards in our geometrical journey, it would be proper to next meet pattern pioneer and lover of nature, German poet and philosopher Johann Wolfgang von Goethe (1749–1832). Among the first to delve deeply into the study of forms and structures within the natural world, Goethe's first major scientific work, *The Metamorphosis of Plants* (1790), is packed with scientific discoveries about similarities that occur within the natural world. He had a supremely creative and curious mind, and was awestruck by nature's ornate orchestration and profound interconnectivity, writing that 'Each creature is but a patterned gradation of one great harmonious whole'.

Again and again nature can be observed to have found the simplest, most energy-efficient way to reproduce and exist, from the organization of leaves in order to allow for the best absorption of light and oxygen, to the cooling cracks of rock formations. Is the Golden Ratio a number so intrinsically embedded within us that our eyes will 'see' when something looks correct? Such questions have entranced philosophers, theologians, ecologists, mathematicians and scientists since the dawn of civilization, and we are still finding inspiring and engaging ways to narrate these important ideas.

'Come forth into the light of things, let Nature be your teacher.'
William Wordsworth (1770–1850), English poet

LEARNING FROM NATURE | REDRESSING BALANCE

The patterns of the natural world are clearly an endless source of inspiration and intrigue, but why does any of this actually matter? Why should we even care about the similarities between the ripples formed on sand dunes and the patterns found on zebra skin?

A whole host of triumphant and breathtaking discoveries have famously had pattern exploration and understanding at their core, and the powerful link between pattern and leaps in human intelligence are hard to ignore. The drive to better understand spontaneous pattern formation has led some of the greatest minds and innovators to link disparate fields of science – from zoology to mechanics, chemical kinetics to sociology. It has required them to work outside of their areas of expertise in new and unexpected ways. For the pioneering British computer scientist Alan Turing (1912–54), it was a jump from pure mathematics into the realms of physics and engineering that led him to create the massive electromagnetic machine able to crack the Enigma code during World War II, an act that likely shortened the war by at least two years and saved millions of lives. It was Turing's interest in logic and pattern that wandered without bounds and allowed him to become the father of computer science and artificial intelligence, despite having no formal laboratory experience.

'What underlies great science is what underlies great art, whether it is visual or written, and that is the ability to distinguish patterns out of chaos.'
Diana Gabaldon (1952–), American novelist

Today the interest in pattern both on and beneath the surface, across many influential disciplines, has never been greater. The research and implementation of pattern need not be confined to the contents of a test tube, the surface of garments on the catwalk or the print inside an envelope. This new direction of thinking about the world in which we live and breathe doesn't simply look to nature for aesthetic enjoyment, but digs much deeper to understand what we can learn from nature to create sustainable solutions that will positively shape the future beyond our own lifetimes – and pattern organization lies at the very heart of many of these solutions.

These perfectly pleated palms are evidence of nature's wisdom and the energy-efficient design that is all around us.

Our man-made systems can lead to chaos. Perhaps it is time to define a new way of being?

DIG DEEPER

CELEBRATE INTERCONNECTIVITY

Amid the many conflicts of the modern world, the need to remember our deep interconnectivity – both to our environment and to each other – has never been more imperative. Sensing connection makes us feel part of a much greater whole and affirms our sense of belonging to something much more permanent than ourselves. Cultivating a feeling of connectivity leads to an increased sense of empathy and compassion.

Top left, Rugged Rocks, Oregon, USA | Top right, Iris Crater, Suren Manvelyan | Bottom left, Mars View, 'Victoria Crater' at Meridiani Planum, Mars | Bottom right, Jaguar Blotches, South America

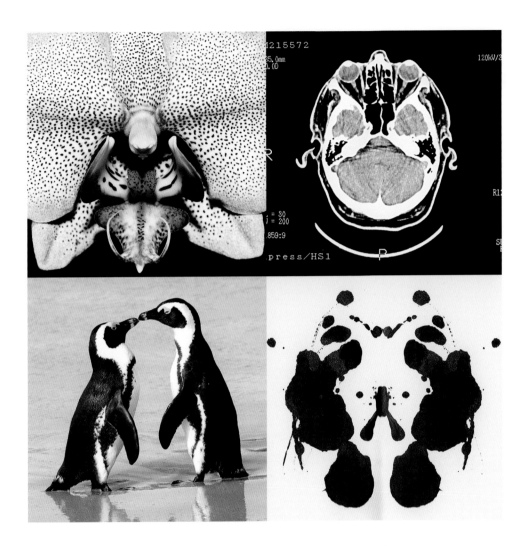

SEEK BALANCE

CONSIDER COINCIDENCE

Whether looking through a microscope or a telescope, the same patterns exist everywhere. Like beacons for our human understanding, we are only just beginning to value the importance of the curious coincidences that abound in the natural world. Whether digging deep or stepping back, we should pause and reflect on the shapes and formations that make up the world around us and have done so for millennia.

Top left, Orchid Butterfly, Himalayas | Top right, Head on View, brain scan | Bottom left, Penguin Pair, Boulders Beach, South Africa Bottom right, Rorschach Form, ink and paper

An excellent example of this approach is the relatively new field popularized by scientist and author Janine Benyus in *Biomimicry: Innovation Inspired by Nature* (1997). Biomimicry looks to nature as the ultimate inspiration, as 'model, measure and mentor'. In a world of overload and excessive waste, biomimicry emphasizes sustainability as the only solution. A surge of interest in this area has become an entire movement where the imitation of the models, systems and elements of nature are explored for the purpose of solving complex human problems. Ideas are already being applied to many different fields, from engineering to education, health to finance; resulting in ceramics that borrow properties from seashells and rubber tyres with treads inspired by the physicality of tree frogs. Individuals and institutions alike are coming together to work on longer-lasting solutions that will create sustainable responses to many of the problems that man has created over the last few centuries.

> *'The great use of life is to spend it for something that will outlast it.'*
> William James (1842–1910), philosopher and psychologist

Iris van Herpen's autumn/winter 2011/12 couture collection was inspired by micro-organisms, suggesting a renewed reverence for the natural world.

Since we launched PATTERNITY we have noticed a steady increase in the interest in the patterns and textures of the natural world both in microscopic and galactic extremes. From fashion designer Christopher Kane's (1982–) printed sweatshirts of bursting supernova to architects Jacques Herzog (1950–) and Pierre de Meuron's (1950–) Beijing National Stadium (2008), inspired by the interlocking woven construction of a bird's nest, and from the Technicolor celebrations of forests painted by British artist David Hockney (1937–) to the collections of Dutch fashion designer Iris van Herpen (1984–), inspired by intricate micro-organisms, there are many examples that traverse disciplines and materials. From research to implementation, the interest in natural patterns, both big and small, is finding a new voice.

Our increasingly urbanized lives are having a major impact on other parts of the world, from the Amazon to the Antarctic, that we might never get to visit.

Beyond our PATTERNITY research, projects and products, we felt it increasingly important to get hands-on, and to connect and collaborate with our PATTERNITY community through experiences and events that take our educational approach to pattern curation offline and into the real world. The full PATTERNITY events programme launched in April 2013 with PATTERN POWER, a cultural festival format that included hands-on workshops, cross-disciplinary talks, film screenings and industry think-tanks that used the commonality of pattern and relationships as a lens through which to analyse important questions about everyday existence in powerful and unexpected ways.

> *'Generating interesting connections between disparate subjects is what makes art so fascinating to create and to view ... we are forced to contemplate a new, higher pattern that binds lower ones together.'*
> Daniel Bor (1975–), neuroscientist and author

PATTERN POWER has since gone on to become the blueprint for an ongoing programme of PATTERNITY events and educational experiences that champion the intersection of the creative arts with the sciences and the natural world. These diverse events, linked through the unique curation of pattern that brings the PATTERNITY ethos and aesthetic into real life, seek to positively shape the future and to drive wide-reaching positive social change at a time when the world needs it most.

HONOURING WISDOM | A TIMELY EVOLUTION

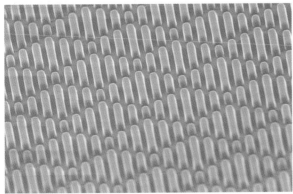

Inspired by the distinct structure of shark skin (top), the Sharklet plastic sheet (above) is a technological coating that can be applied to surfaces in hospitals, for example, to reduce the growth of harmful bacteria.

The impact of our unsustainable patterns of behaviour is visible from outer space, as seen in this aerial photo of American farmland.

Research into biomimicry, ecology and sustainability is coming to define a wider reaching cultural shift. It is now startlingly evident that nature is not a resource from which we can endlessly extract. Fortunately it appears that humankind is beginning to think about our place *within* rather than *atop* the natural world. Instead of seeing nature as a resource to dominate and exploit, we are entering a new era that seeks to learn about nature's complexity, wisdom and innate efficiency, through respect, co-operation and dialogue rather than through domination or control. This way of thinking and learning honours 3.8 billion years of evolution, and sees our mere 200,000 years of human life not as superior, but as deeply interconnected. As we are living increasingly urbanized lives it is becoming all the more important to remind ourselves of this strong link we have with the natural world.

From the expert arrangements of honeybees – timeless symbols of industry and efficiency – carefully crafting their hexagonal honeycombs to provide the maximum storage from the minimum amount of building material, to the expert branching of our own circulatory and respiratory systems, it seems that we have an awful lot to learn from nature. We can no longer think of nature and all of its wonders as being something separate from us.

> *'Ultimately – there are no parts at all. What we call a part is merely a pattern in an inseparable web of relationships.'*
> Fritjof Capra (1939–), physicist

This holistic way of seeing the world is about recognizing relationships; something that was fundamental to the way social scientist Gregory Bateson observed the natural world. His interaction with nature was so intensely felt that he would describe the beauty manifest in the complexity of nature's patterned relationships – with all his being. Whether surveying the similarities of a crustacean's claw with the petals of a primrose, his boundless approach was clearly not just about scientific discovery; it also spoke considerably of the mental and emotional effects of direct interaction with nature and all its variations. This way of seeing is most evident today in the field of deep ecology, which pioneers the core belief that the living environment as a whole should be respected, with human relationships working in balance with nature. Beyond its place as a beneficial human resource the natural world should have the legal right to live and flourish. In addition, since we are living increasingly urbanized lives, it is all the more important to remind ourselves of the strong link we have with the natural world – and to use nature as a guide to inform future strategies.

> *'To work our way towards a shared and living language once again, we must first learn how to discover patterns which are deep, and capable of generating life.'*
> Christopher Alexander (1936–), architect
> and co-creator of A Pattern Language (1977)

161

Polymath César Manrique's *Monumento al Campesino* explores the profound harmony between man-made design and the natural landscape.

Patterns are literally interwoven with the values of Native Americans. It's time to look back in order to move forward.

This is a similar mind-set to that of the Spanish artist, architect and activist César Manrique (1919–92) regarding the protection of the Canary Islands in the 1970s. Manrique saw the volcanic island of Lanzarote as a microcosm that mirrored the wider world, which was becoming increasingly homogenized by globalization and human greed. During the final years of his life in the 1990s, César kept notebooks recording fragments of thoughts and his innermost convictions and social aims – in particular those concerned with creativity and our universal connection with nature. He spoke of the importance of striving for balance, of the need for mankind to live in harmony with the natural world. In 2014 we led a 'PATTERNITRIP' to Lanzarote. There we explored Manrique's key philosophies reflected in his various sculptures, paintings, buildings and parks that are dotted around the island. Manrique strongly upheld the importance of 'promoting the characteristic differences of every place on the planet'. In a world being stripped of all cultural differences, heritage and wisdom he saw 'the perfection and balance of nature as the wisest lesson possible for man'. It is through this more mindful approach that we can hope to understand our own part of a much bigger picture within the natural world. At PATTERNITY we truly believe that the time spent musing about what's growing in our back garden or sitting on the end of our fork can yield small but wide-reaching change.

> *'To know the order of nature and regard the universe as orderly is the highest function of the mind.'*
> Baruch Spinoza (1632–1677), Dutch philosopher

A SUSTAINABLE FUTURE | CONTENTED CONNECTION

In a Western world obsessed by separate parts, mechanisms, materials and newness, there is a comforting side effect to feeling integrated into something reassuringly infinite. Feeling part of an interconnected whole has the power to bring about a more enduring contentment and shape the way we engage with physical and emotional environments. As we begin to feel integrated on both individual and collective plains, we become more aware of our deep connectivity with nature. We cannot help but treat the natural world and its contents with more respect – for it is a part of us, and us a part of it. We become more mindful of only taking as much as we *need*, as opposed to *want*. This is a mind-set that kicks back against the growth-orientated and globalized culture that currently dominates most of the world and changes our wider patterns of thinking and doing. With a focus on nature and sustainability, we feel united with our fellow citizens of Earth, working with nature not against it – an approach that links some of the oldest civilizations from the Ancient Egyptians to Native Americans. There seems to be a notable link between the regard for nature and sustainability, not only with regard to resources but also to the endurance of entire species.

> *'I live on Earth at present, and I don't know what I am. I know that I am not a category. I am not a thing – a noun. I seem to be a verb, an evolutionary process – an integral function of the universe.'*
> R Buckminster Fuller (1895–1983), architect

When we first started PATTERNITY we had a very visual conception of pattern. The PATTERNITY image archive and studio projects remain important windows into the PATTERNITY aesthetic and ethos, but today our research and curation of pattern delves beneath the surface through editorial projects, educational events and live experiences that use pattern to encourage a more in-depth understanding and engagement with the world around us. We are building a growing online community that extends into real-life investigations. From the fun to the fascinating, our events encourage individual and collective examinations of the ways in which the world is or isn't working.

PATTERNITY events serve as in-depth and engaging explorations as to how both visible and non-visible patterns affect our lives and how they can be engaged to positively shape the future. Whether working in collaboration with brands, institutions or the public, our ethos of 'using pattern to encourage a more positive connection to our environment and each other' brings together our growing network of pattern specialists – from the worlds of art and design to music, science, technology, nature, health, psychology, environment, ecology and beyond. Starting in London, where PATTERNITY began, we are spreading our ethos further as ambassadors from all over the world begin to host their own PATTERNITY events in urban and rural communities around the globe.

Our journey of exploration has only just begun.

From Nigeria to New York, documenting patterns within both the man-made and the natural world has become a core part of our practice.

Looking at the natural world through a new lens, such as Olafur Eliasson's *Viewing Machine* at Inhotim Contemporary Art Museum, Brazil, holds the key to a more sustainable and happy future.

Pages 164—5, Road Shapes, Ivan Shaw, Perth, Australia

Left, Rusty Rivers, Bernhard Edmaier, Laguna Roja, Chile | Right, Hair Slithers, Georges Antoni

Page 168, Dune Movement, Jeremy Woodhouse, Merzouga, Morocco | Page 169, Sleek Shoulder Shine, SCANDEBERGS

Page 170, Bubble Universe, Neil Watson, detergent on black

'No man is an island entire of itself; every man is a piece of the continent, a part of the main.'

John Donne (1572–1631), poet

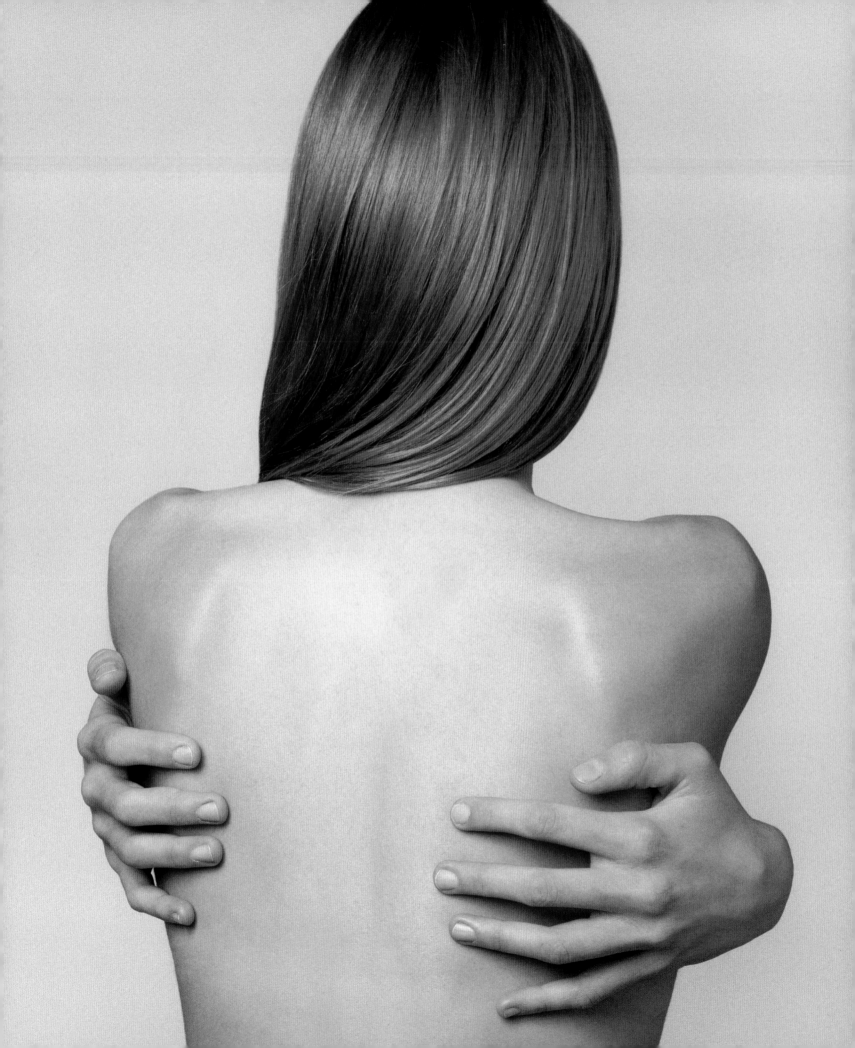

PATTERN FOCUS

#HEXAGON #CELL #POLYGON #TESSELATE

A hexagon can be mathematically playful in the way that it can allow for regular multiples and divisions of itself. Numerically, a hexad is both the sum of its first three integers, one and their multiple, qualifying it as the first perfect number in integer-based mathematics.

Translating the numeracy of the hexagon into the geometry of their honeycomb, honeybees instinctively arrange it into hexagonal shapes. After the triangle and the square, the hexagon is the final regular polygon that tessellates perfectly through its own shape, so not only does it provide an efficient means of storage and organization, it also structurally supports regular multiplications and divisions of itself.

Benzene carries a ubiquitous role in our everyday lives for just this reason. This elegant hexagonal chemical-compound structure, composed of hydrogen and carbon atoms, is arranged in ways that make it an indispensable component of some of the structures of everyday substances and materials, such as paracetamol or the plastics that we have made part of our daily lives.

Hexagons are also structurally visible in snowflakes, graphite and some six-legged insects. Even when invisible, hexagons are among some of the strongest building blocks to chemical and physical structures. Carbon nanotubes (CNTs), made of hexagonal cylindrical mesh, are the strongest material yet known, sustaining a weight equivalent to 6,422kg-force on a cable with a cross section of $1mm^2$, making them hundreds of times stronger than steel but six times lighter. This combined strength and low density has given rise to a multitude of innovations, from forming parts of sports gear to contributing to bone tissue engineering and formation. Strong yet light, and capable of regular assembly, the hexagon's versatility makes it a very modern symbol of enterprise and efficiency.

Top left, Hex-Ray Vision, sunglasses: Hussein Chalayan | Top right, Sud Cells, soap bubbles
Middle left, Honeycomb Hangings, Quince Honey Farm, Devon | Middle right, Hexadome, The Eden
Project, Cornwall | Bottom left, Bolted Brass, brass nuts | Bottom right, Scale Structure
Skin, albino boa constrictor

Page 174, Volcanic Shore, PATTERNITY, El Golfo, Lanzarote | Page 175, Sulphur Explorer, Willem Jaspert, Iceland

Left, Moss Mounds, Katarzyna Pilipionek, lava field, Iceland | Right, Fashion Fuzz, fashion: Céline

'Nature, that universal and public manuscript.'

Sir Thomas Browne (1605–1682), English polymath and author

Left, Phytoplankton Swirl, NASA Goddard Space Flight Center/USGS, Baltic Sea

Right, Space Suit, Andrew Vowles, fashion: Berthold

'Ultimately – there are no parts at all. What we call a part is merely a pattern in an inseparable web of relationships.'

Fritjof Capra (1939–), Austrian-born American physicist
and founding director of the Center for Ecoliteracy in Berkeley, California

PATTERN FOCUS

#CRACK #MARBLE #ANGULAR #FACET

Cracks are patterns that occur because of a feedback process provided by interactions between neighbouring cracks and the environment. Not only are they self-organizing, despite appearing random and fractured, but they also allow growth, as they express the elasticity of the form they're being made through. Cracks reveal pathways that have been created by the release of a build-up of tension, whether they appear in parched earth or as hairline cracks on ceramics.

Chinese narratives place great aesthetic value in the craze-patterns on their pottery, noticing their relationship to tectonic force lines, fractal patterns of river networks and other forms of naturally occurring crack lines. Resulting features of cracked outlines appear random, but are in fact ordered by a fractal patterning of events, where what has happened in the past helps to determine what happens next.

Fractography is the study of fractures or cracks in materials, and is often used to predict causes of possible failure in a structure. The cracks on cement, the hairline fractures on iPhones or the cracks on the surface crust of bread embody a different type of meaning when looked at through the lens of their own material. They make visible the always-present relationship of a material and the way its environment has grown to shape it and continues to be shaped by it.

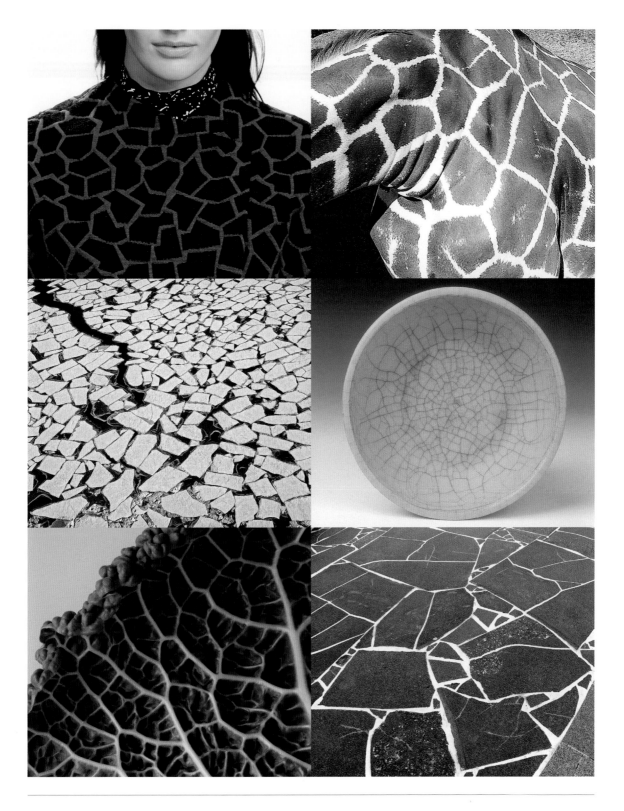

Top left, Cracked Up, fashion: Proenza Schouler | Top right, Geo Giraffe, Ramat Gan, Israel | Middle left, Ice Path, Disco Bay, Greenland | Middle right, Crackle Glaze, 13th Century Southern Song Dynasty, China | Bottom left, Green Network, Savoy cabbage | Bottom right, Crazed Paving, Melbourne

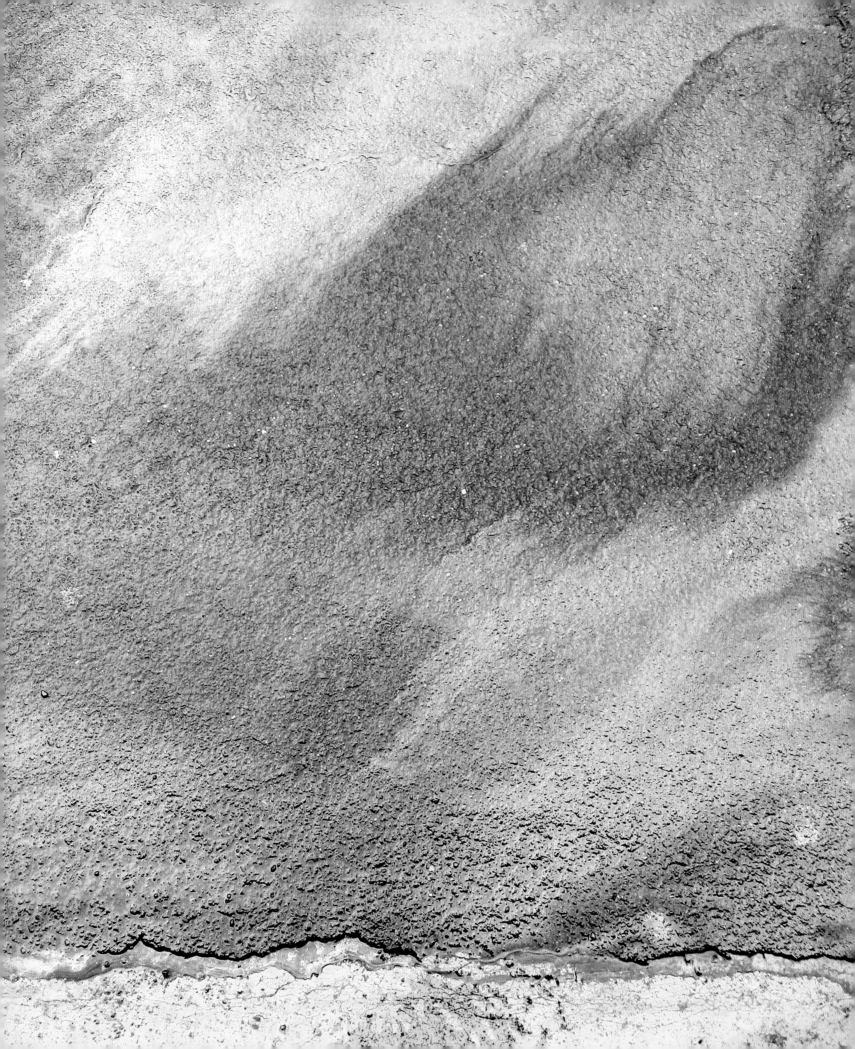

Page 182, Rainbow Road, Piers Rutterford, London | Page 183, Technicolour Tresses, Mark Pillai, fashion: Blumarine

Left, Water Wiggle, PATTERNITY, Museo César Manrique, Lanzarote | Right, Holographic Walk, ImaxTree, fashion: Hussein Chalayan

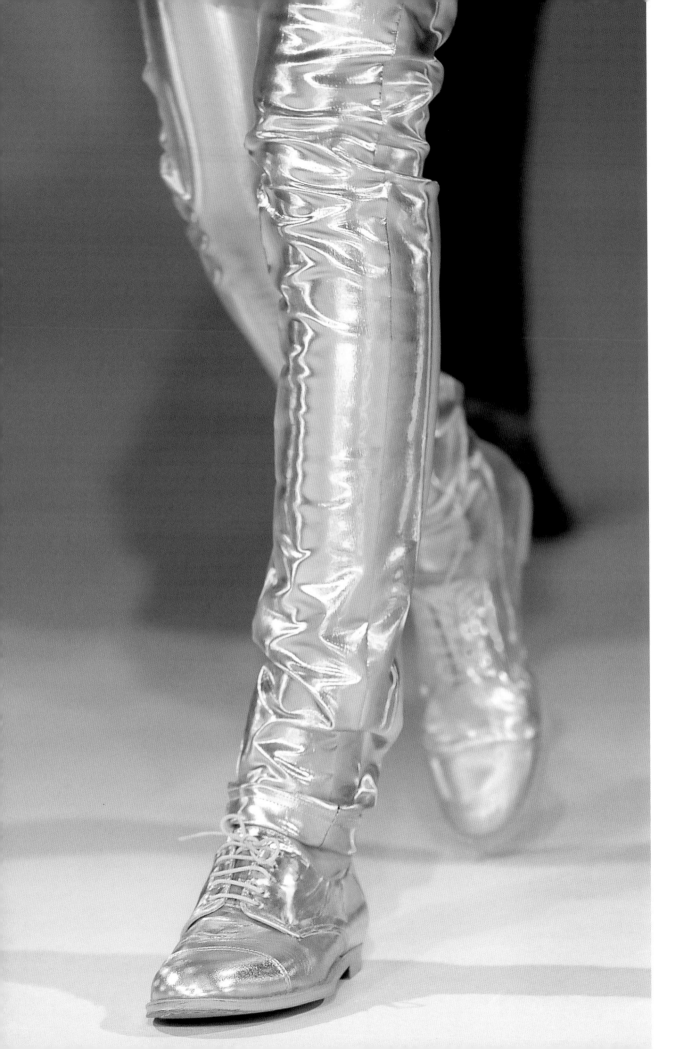

'We are like islands in the sea, separate on the surface but connected in the deep.'

william James (1842–1910), philosopher and psychologist

PATTERN FOCUS

#WAVE #RIPPLE #CONTOUR #CREASE

Whether they are aeolian (wind-formed) or, in the case of shore patterns, created by the compound effects of currents, wind and tide, the wave's character is strongly influenced by particular local conditions. The wave, whether seen or unseen, beautifully represents movement and the transferral of energy.

Sand granules are in themselves inert, but when wind is blown across them, they form ripple patterns that mimic the effect of movement, like wind rippling the surface of water. Sand ripples are intriguing because they are formed through a feedback process that makes visible, small, random irregularities that when aggregated reveal a self-made environmental tapestry that is a reflection of the forces in nature. From sand dunes in the Sahara to the surface of Mars, some of nature's flow patterns can be seen apparently 'frozen in time' as ripples in places devoid of water – a universal pattern formation found both here on Earth and in the reaches of the known solar system.

Invisible waves are at the heart of our visual and auditory senses too; light waves and sound waves give form to what we can see and what we can hear. The range of the waves that are accessible to human sight and hearing shape the world that we perceive and make up part of what it is to be alive: to communicate. Bats are capable of receiving a much higher pitch of sound waves in order to navigate their surroundings in the dark. Whales are similarly capable of producing low-frequency sounds that in turn make it possible for them to locate the position of food sources underwater. Waves are constantly at work around us, in both microscopic and macroscopic scales across the universe.

Page 188, Painted Swirl, Neil Watson, paint on paper | Page 189, Shrouded Smoke, Mel Bles, fashion: Derek Lawlor

Top left, Scribble Stance, fashion: Michael Griffin | Top right, Whale Wave, pilot whale, Tenerife | Middle left, Car Crunch, Italy | Middle right, Window Waves, Australia Bottom left, Water Planes, Margate, England | Bottom right, Indigo Folds, screen print

Left, Meat Marble, PATERNITY + Neil Watson, steak | Right, Material Mash Up, Kate Jackling, set: Lightning + Kinglyface

Pages 192–3, Crack Down, PATERNITY, Nevada Desert, USA

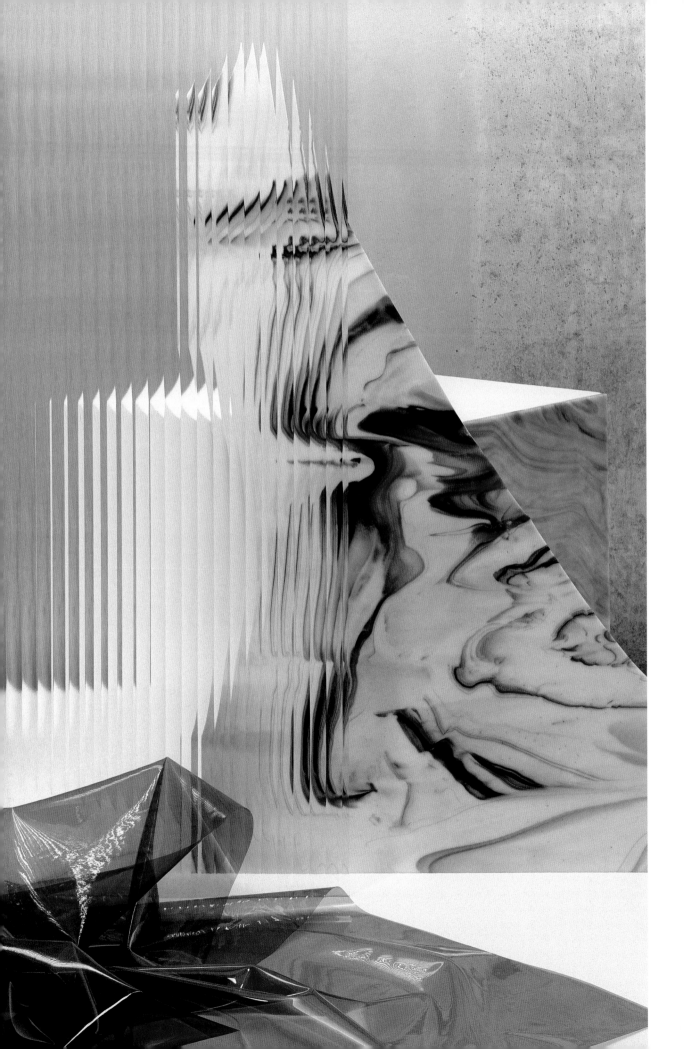

'What underlies great science is what underlies great art, whether it is visual or written, and that is the ability to distinguish patterns out of chaos.'

Diana Gabaldon (1952–), American novelist

PATTERN FOCUS

#BRANCH #FRACTAL #MEANDER

Branches are poetic in the way they can both describe and make visible a process by revealing a structure. Branching patterns are abundant throughout nature and science, from the Purkinje (neuron cells) of human brains to the meandering patterns of lightning strikes and river networks. Branches are typically fractals that follow naturally formed and locally structured processes. For example, the geological process of landscape erosion is responsible for the branching of river networks, where the flow of water not only carves out the landscape into particular patterns, but also becomes the source of pattern itself.

Whether a branching pattern is distributing 'inwardly' (rivers), 'outwardly' (trees) or in both directions (lightning strikes), the process always involves finer and finer ramifications, suggesting that the system of the branching structure is in constant flux. The Romanesco broccoli takes a shape born from fractal patterns similar to those found in the branching of trees but growing outwardly in striking three-dimensional spirals. Branching patterns are crucial in supporting life: without the subtle systems to transport water, oxygen, nutrients or electrical impulses to delicate and dynamic parts of the body, life would simply not exist.

These natural branching and fractal patterns serve to highlight the intuition of nature, always knowing the most effective methods of distribution and growth. The more we explore such patterns, natural or man-made, the more we can see the connectivity of everything around us. This inseparable affinity with life, deep within our bodies and outside them, can be both soothing and relaxing to observe.

Top left, Tree Top, fashion: Proenza Schouler | Top right, Energy Forks, New Mexico, USA | Middle left, Breathing Branches, lung x-ray | Middle right, Meandering Mountains, Death Valley, USA | Bottom left, Hand Holds, painted hands | Bottom right, Pastel Fractals, Lincolnshire, England

Left, Jelly Domes, Lionel Cironneau, Oceanographic Museum of Monaco | Right, Draped in Dots, Paul Maffi

'Everything is interwoven and the web is holy.'

Marcus Aurelius (AD121–180), philosopher, Roman emperor

PATTERN FOCUS

#BLOTCH #DAPPLE #FLECK #SPECKLE

Whether detected in animal camouflage or the clusters of villages, towns or cities around the globe, blotches are universal and familiar forms that we can find in much natural phenomena. Magmatic rock shows blotches in the rawest case of formation on the Earth. Blotches are a visual noise that help to preserve some continuity with one's environment. They also alert us to something out of the ordinary.

In busy natural environments, animals are born with patches on their skin in order to hide among the muddled pattern of foliage and nature; the eggs of most ground-nesting birds blend with their surroundings to protect them from predators. Blotches can also be bold: the skin-patterns of different frogs and toads provide particularly rich fields of blotches in a huge range of colours, and different types of fish have blotches to mark variation across species, with similar distinction techniques found across many aspects of the animal kingdom.

Blotches also exist as part of the physical description of our own human bodies. Our skin can be described as clear, freckled or patchy, with distinctive types of blotches carrying different polarizing meanings. To be patchy is indicative of a possible illness or condition that needs attention. To be densely freckled, is to be considered both aesthetically unusual and beautiful.

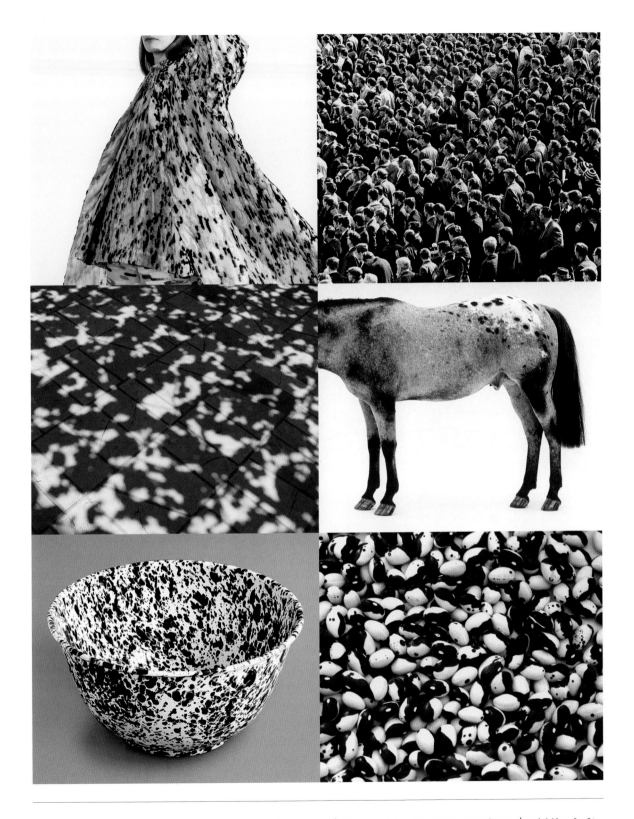

Top left, Flecked Flair, fashion: Satu Maaranen | Top right, Crowded Craniums | Middle left, Gestalt Floor, Croatia | Middle right, Pony Patches, Appaloosa horse | Bottom left, Serving Splatter, enamel bowl | Bottom right, Blotched Beans, orca beans

Left, Flamingo Flecks, Michael Poliza, Lake Bogoria, Kenya | Right, Full On Fur, Brendan Freeman, hat: Beyond Retro, jacket: Rellik

'Come forth into the light of things, let Nature be your teacher.'

William Wordsworth (1770–1850), English poet

PATTERN IS LIFE | A CONTINUATION

A NEW WAY OF BEING

'One cannot lead a life that is truly excellent without feeling that one belongs to something greater and more permanent than oneself.'

Mihaly Csikszentmihalyi (1934–), psychologist and author

While Christopher Columbus and Charles Darwin were limited to earthly explorations, the technological and scientific advancements of the 20th century have created new paths for exciting discoveries on both macro and micro scales. The entire universe has been flung open for our perusal and our sense of perspective has skyrocketed along with it. Viewed from outer space, the Earth is a glittering ball of energetic connections – a sparkling web of life. New discoveries are constantly being made and there are fewer and fewer unexplored patches of dark.

Our limitless desire to venture into and discover more about unchartered territories is a remarkable quality of humankind, and yet this spirit of exploration has been inextricably linked with the mercenary quest for ownership and political power throughout history. The space race, for example, between the USA and the then Soviet Union in the fifties and sixties was fundamentally a competition for supremacy, symbolizing technical superiority, economic potency and governmental might. However amid the global television broadcasts and bravado, the flashes and flags, the human sense of awe and wonder was not lost. Many astronauts (some 500 to date) who have observed planet Earth in orbit have reported that the experience brings about a significant cognitive shift and reordered sense of perspective. On contemplating the

giant sphere – the floating orb that houses everything we have ever created, ever loved or ever lost, representing the beginning and the end of everything we have ever known – the astronauts described recognizing the Earth as our collective home as if for the very first time. Edgar D Mitchell (1930–), Commander of the Apollo 14 mission in 1971, described 'an overwhelming sense of oneness, of connectedness; it wasn't "them and us", it was "that's me"; that's all of it, it's ... it's one thing.' We have these pioneers, among many others, to thank not only for a scientific revolution, but also for the advancement of humanity. We are living, working and thinking as a result of these discoveries today.

Today a quick internet search can generate hundreds of pictures of the Earth in orbit and it is hard for us to imagine that only a few decades ago we had no concept of how our planet looked from afar. The unmanned Lunar Orbiter 1 sent back the first grainy images of the Earth in 1966, but it would be American astronaut William Anders' (1933–) stunning *Earthrise* photograph, taken in 1968 during the Apollo 8 mission, that caused a dramatic shift in our understanding. The picture – which captures the Earth rising behind the surface of the moon, a green and blue swirling marble shielded only by a paper-thin atmosphere from the black abyss beyond – has been described as the most influential environmental photograph of all time. *Earthrise* was perhaps only surpassed by images returned from Voyager 1 in 1990 that show the Earth, a swirling marbled sphere, from a distance of 6 billion km (3¾ billion miles), leading the astrophysicist and author Carl Sagan (1934–1996) to coin the phrase 'pale blue dot'.

The philosopher Frank White has explored the cognitive shift experienced by the astronauts in more depth in *The Overview Effect: Space Exploration and Human Evolution* (1987). He found that astronauts reported a newfound clarity, comparable only to a spiritual experience, when they observed how fragile yet connected the Earth seems from this perspective. From outer space, national boundaries seemed to vanish, the conflicts that divide us became less relevant and the need to celebrate our universal commonality not only became clear, but also crucial. The astronauts appeared to experience *ubuntu* – a Nguni Bantu term, originating from South Africa, which roughly translates as 'humanity, fellow feeling or kindness'. It is often used in a more philosophical sense to mean 'a universal bond that connects all humanity', which also captures the important experience of feeling a part of a much greater, united whole.

The overview effect has been the subject of much interest from film-makers, philosophers and scientists alike because this new way of seeing has the potential for wider-reaching cultural change. Back down on Earth we are living in a time of great contradiction. We are constantly connected but many lack a true sense of community or contentment. Our lives and landscapes are becoming increasingly homogenized and indistinguishable, yet at the same time disparate communities suffer food, water and energy shortages as well as outbreaks of conflicts or disease. There has never been a more critical time in human history for us to start feeling and acting together as a united, global community. We are so flooded with commodities that we have lost a sense of authenticity.

For many urbanites, the night sky is more of an orange fog that shrouds the city than a portal to any greater cosmic connection. Humanity has ventured far and wide both on the Earth and into the known universe – but in many ways we are still lost. We have become so absorbed by the ebb and flow of everyday life that we forget to step back and meditate on the bigger picture that is largely out of view. There is no universal handbook with which to guide our actions and judge our achievements. An age of bombardment of information, imagery and distractions has wiped our collective awareness and understanding of one of the most fundamental languages that unites us all. It is a language we need to learn anew.

Although patterns make up the fabric of our universe, their majesty is rarely engagingly reported. Many schools and educational institutions might teach us to repeat the sequence of the Fibonacci numbers or test our ability to memorize geometry facts, but pupils are seldom encouraged to marvel (as the ancients once did) at how these numbers and shapes miraculously manifest themselves throughout life. Similarly, from catwalk to high street, gallery to bathroom floor, prints and patterns adorn our homes and wardrobes but we have become numb to their deeper beauty and greater meaning beyond the surface. We have lost sight of the immense and humbling power of pattern to unite worlds, to guide our human endeavours and to create more sustainable, happier lives full of joy and wonder.

We are in danger of losing the sense of awe that drove Archimedes, Copernicus and Galileo to better understand our place within the universe, or urged the likes of Benjamin Franklin, Marie Curie and Tim Berners-Lee to define new ways for us to live in it. Instead we have grown to favour the immediate gratification of bite-sized information, passing trends and physical possessions. Social media constantly asks us to break down complex ideas into 140 characters or forces us to encapsulate complicated belief systems into one single photograph. It is time to break this pattern.

On the surface, patterns and markings are a visual display; they help us navigate, establish who we are and signify our role within a group. But they are also part of the very fabric of our being. From the electrical wave impulses of our brains to the tempo of our heartbeats, pattern is profoundly entrenched within us. Humankind must take comfort in the symmetry and structure in these recurring rhythms and repetitions that are both seen and unseen. These are the patterns that shape the whole of our universe. We are connected to each other and to the world around us in a way that is enduring and vast, and this realization has the power to positively change the way we feel about the world. It can empower us and bring about a timely shift of perspective at both local and global levels.

We are living in a time of great transformation. A time where we are beginning to question every part of the system that shapes the world we share. The ancient mathematical philosophers described the integration of pattern as *harmonia mundi*, 'harmony of the world'. Years later we are living through a time of great discord. However, as we begin to emerge and learn from a competitive age challenged by fragmentation, there is a newfound sense of comfort in the realization that life isn't compartmentalized and chaotic, but an expertly ordered and interconnected web. It is both humbling and timely to remember that nature, filled with infinitely inspiring patterns, has its own way of finding balance.

There are numerous simple, universal solutions to the problems of our time just waiting to be discovered. Businesswoman and writer Margaret Heffernan (1955–) argues that the biggest threats we face are those we don't see – not because they are secret or invisible, but because we are 'wilfully blind'. Should we wish to open up to new ways of seeing – and also being – we have the opportunity to delve deeper than we ever have before, to spend more of our time exploring the bigger, worthwhile questions as we begin to pick up the ancient threads that for so long

have been severed from our collective and connected consciousness. It is time that we begin to learn from the wise and powerful patterns that surround us all.

Our collective future is resting on our will to become more aware, to co-operate and cross-pollinate ideas and skills – and to remember our deep connectivity both to each other and to the natural world. We need to celebrate the commonalities that unite us all. Our ability to detect and appreciate patterns big or small, regardless of discipline, is fast becoming one of the most important skills in aiding us to develop and enhance our understanding of our world and beyond.

This book marks both an ending and a new beginning for PATTERNITY. As an organization we are still evolving and finding new ways to promote the power of pattern.

Inspiration remains everywhere. We just need to see it.

Pages 206–7, Curtain Call, Tim Gutt, draped fabric

'When patterns are broken, new worlds emerge.'

Tuli Kupferberg (1923–2010), counterculture poet, singer, cartoonist and publisher

Page 208, Harlequin Shrimp, Luiz A. Rocha, Bali, Indonesia | Page 209, Camo Couture, Ben Weller, fashion: Michael Kors

Left, Palm Springs, Sofie Hermans, Barcelona | Right, Fan Flare, Ahmet Unver

Page 212, Wonderwave, PATTERNITY, Ilha Grande, Brazil | Page 213, Drape Drench, Patric Shaw, crêpe voile

'There is not a fragment in all nature, for every relative fragment of one thing is a full harmonious unit in itself.'

John Muir (1838–1914), naturalist and author

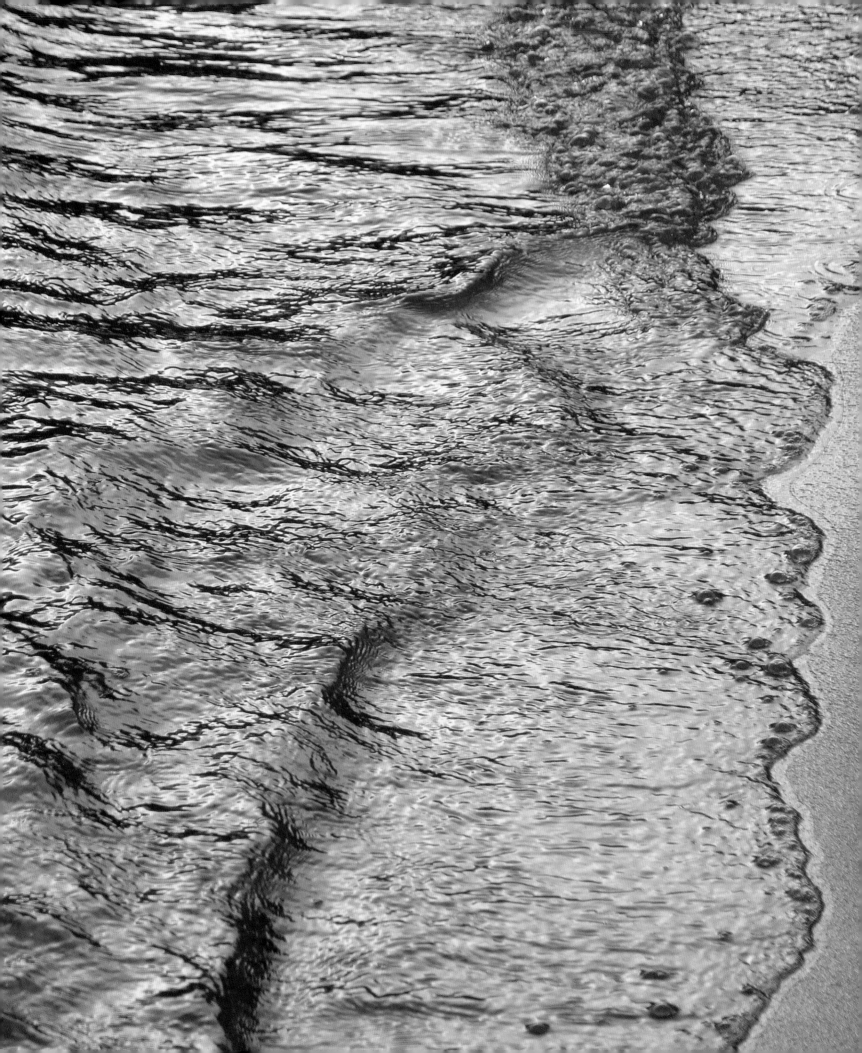

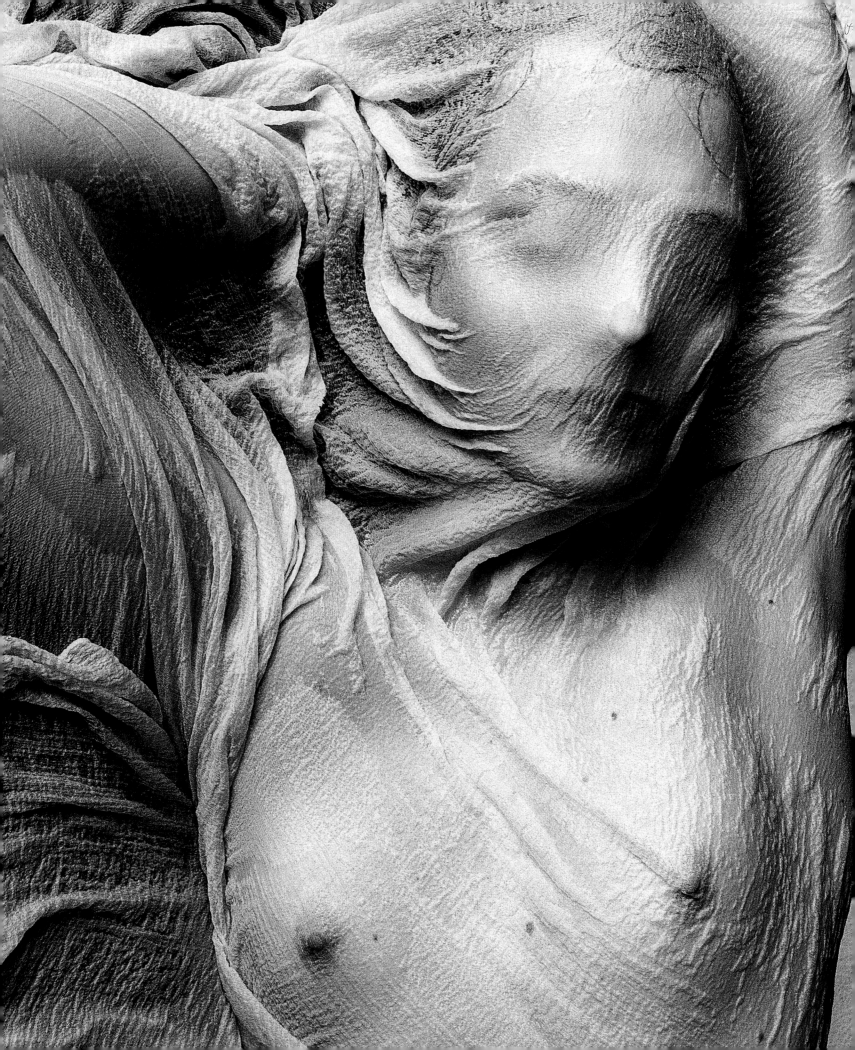

FURTHER READING

'If there is something you know, communicate it.
If there is something you don't know, search for it.'
Engraving from *Encyclopédie: Truth* (1772)

To explore the many themes at the core of our organization further, we suggest working through the list below, which includes many of the brilliant works – and minds – that have helped us to form *PATTERNITY: A New Way Of Seeing*.

A Beginner's Guide to Constructing the Universe (2003) Michael S Schneider
A Whole New Mind: Why Right-Brainers Will Rule the Future (2005) Daniel H Pink
Art Forms in Nature (1998) Ernst Haeckel
Biomimicry: Innovation Inspired by Nature (1997) Janine M Benyus
Breakfast With Socrates: A Day with the World's Greatest Minds (2010) Robert
        Rowland Smith
Communicating with Pattern: Circles and Dots (2006) Mark Hampshire and
        Keith Stephenson
Communicating with Pattern: Squares, Checks, and Grids (2008) Mark Hampshire and
        Keith Stephenson
Communicating with Pattern: Stripes (2006) Mark Hampshire and Keith Stephenson
Designa: Technical Secrets of the Traditional Visual Arts (2014) Adam Tetlow, Daud
        Sutton, Lisa DeLong, Scott Olsen, David Wade, Phoebe McNaughton
Diary: A Novel (2003) Chuck Palahniuk (quote reprinted by permission of Donadio & Olson, Inc.)
Finding Flow: The Psychology of Engagement with Everyday Life (1998)
        Mihaly Csikszentmihalyi
Herd: How to Change Mass Behaviour by Harnessing Our True Nature (2007) Mark Earls
How to Thrive in the Digital Age (The School of Life) (2012) Tom Chatfield
I Seem to Be a Verb: Environment and Man's Future (1970) R Buckminster Fuller
Li: Dynamic Form in Nature (2007) David Wade
Liber Abaci (1202) Leonardo of Pisa
Mind and Nature: A Necessary Unity (1979) Gregory Bateson
Nature's Patterns: A Tapestry in Three Parts (2009) Philip Ball
On the Origin of Species (1859) Charles Darwin
Pale Blue Dot: A Vision of the Human Future in Space (1994) Carl Sagan
Patterns in Nature (1974) Peter S Stevens
Peace is Every Step: The Path of Mindfulness in Everyday Life (1991) Thích Nhất Hạnh

Quadrivium: Number Geometry Music Heaven (2010) Miranda Lundy, Daud Sutton, Anthony Ashton, Jason Martineau, John Martineau

Religion for Atheists: A Non-believer's Guide to the Uses of Religion (2012) Alain de Botton

Sacred Geometry (1998) Miranda Lundy

The Assayer (Italian: *Il Saggiatore*) (1623) Galileo Galilei

The Decorative Art of Today (1925) Le Corbusier

The Fractal Geometry of Nature (1982) Benoît Mandelbrot

The Golden Section (2006) Scott Olsen

The Human Face Of Big Data (2012) Rick Smolan and Jennifer Erwitt

The Marriage of Heaven and Hell (1790) William Blake

The Master and his Emissary: The Divided Brain and the Making of the Western World (2009) Iain McGilchrist

The Metamorphosis of Plants (1790) Johann Wolfgang von Goethe

The Mindful Manifesto: How Doing Less and Noticing More Can Help Us Thrive in a Stressed-out World (2012) Dr Jonty Heaversedge and Ed Halliwell

The Overview Effect: Space Exploration and Human Evolution (1987) Frank White

The Power of Now: A Guide to Spiritual Enlightenment (1997) Eckhart Tolle

The Proper Study of Mankind: An Anthology of Essays (1998) Isaiah Berlin

The Psychopath Test: A Journey Through the Madness Industry (2011) Jon Ronson

The Ravenous Brain: How the New Science of Consciousness Explains Our Insatiable Search for Meaning (2012) Daniel Bor

The Responsible Company: What We've Learned from Patagonia's First 40 Years (2012) Yvon Chouinard and Vincent Stanley

The Rise of the Creative Class: And How it's Transforming Work, Leisure, Community, and Everyday Life (2002) Richard Florida

The Structure of Scientific Revolutions (1962) Thomas S Kuhn

The Timeless Way of Building (1979) Christopher Alexander (quote reprinted by permission of Oxford University Press, USA)

The Use of Lateral Thinking (1967) Edward de Bono

The Web of Life: A New Scientific Understanding of Living Systems (1996) Fritjof Capra

Wabi-Sabi: For Artists, Designers, Poets & Philosophers (1994) Leonard Koren

Walden; or, Life in the Woods (1854) Henry David Thoreau

JOIN US

'Only connect.'

E. M. Forster (1879–1970)

Championing a new way of seeing is a bold ambition. Having started as just two people with a large collection of photographs in a small basement in East London, we now have a global network of more than 1.5 million. This we take as a hopeful sign that our belief in the inspirational power of pattern is evolving into something truly tangible.

This book marks the end of one chapter and the beginning of a new phase.

PATTERNITY exists to connect the dots. We rely on our global network of contributors and collaborators, and on the support of our subscribers. If you would like to get in touch with us, whether it is to find out more about anything featured in the pages of this book, to learn how to work with us on a future project, product or event, or to tell us about your own pattern-focused idea, cause or innovation, we would love to hear from you.

Join us and our glistening web of pattern pioneers at WWW.PATTERNITY.ORG.

You can also connect with us on Facebook, Instagram, Tumblr and Twitter.

IMAGE CREDITS

Page 4, Vent Lines, Photography: PATTERNITY, Sydney, 2011

Page 5, Mono Man, Photography: Mark Pillai, *10 Men*, 2009, Model: Arthur Daniyarov @ Nevs Model/Scouting One by Jon Viatge

Page 6, Palm Streamers, Photography: PATTERNITY, India, 2013

Page 7, Gold Drapes, Sculpture: Kevin Francis Gray, 'Face-Off', 2007

Page 8, Technicolour Weave, Painting: Bernard Frize, 'Caisse', 1997

Page 9, Trellis Trousers, Photography: Nik Hartley, *USED*, SS13, Model: Charon Cooijmans @ Viva

Page 10, Mountain Pleats, Photography: PATTERNITY, Himalayas, 2011,

Page 11, Creased Collection, Photography: Nicolas Coulomb, Études Lookbook, AW14, Model: Fernando Cabral @ Marilyn Hommes

Pages 20-21, Quarry Block Out, Photography: Georges Antoni, Bombo Quarry, Australia, 2011, Model: Ollie Henderson, Creative Direction: PATTERNITY

Page 24, Rectangle Repeat, Photography: PATTERNITY, Rio de Janeiro, Brazil, 2014

Page 25, Conscious Cloth, Photography: Sarah Piantadosi, Conscious Cloth Collection, AW13, Model: Kriss Barupa @ IMG, Styling: Ellie Grace Cumming @ Streeters, Creative Direction: PATTERNITY

Page 26, Shutter Chevrons, Photography: PATTERNITY, East London, 2010

Page 27, Line Lady, Photography: Rory DCS, *Miami Vice*, 2011, Model: Becky @ Premier Model Management, Styling: PATTERNITY

Page 28, Cable Spray, Photography: PATTERNITY, Anzac Bridge, Sydney, 2011

Page 29, Tassel Triangle, Photography: Amy Gwatkin, *Dazed Digital*, Central St Martins MA 2012 Exclusive, Model: Vanusa @ FM London, Styling: Nelma Lakonji

Page 30 top, Galaxy Glass, Photography: PATTERNITY, 2015

Page 30 bottom, Geometric Shelter, Umbrella: David David, 2015

Page 31 top, Koch Snowflake, Diagram: Public Domain

Page 31 bottom left, Cumulus Cluster, Photography: PATTERNITY, Hong Kong, 2012

Page 32 bottom right, Cauliflower Clumps, Photography: PATTERNITY, 2015

Page 32 top, 'Principal Elements of Sacred Geometry', diagram by Freddy Silva

Page 32 bottom, Spaghetti Style, Photography: Lyndon Fawcett-Fright, London, 2012

Page 33 top, Mandarinfish, Photography: Ruth Petzold/Getty Images

Page 33 bottom, Spaghetti Junction, Photography: Mark A. Paulda/Getty Images

Page 34 top left, Shadow Steps, Photography: PATTERNITY, London, 2012

Page 34 top right, Crackle Scape, Photography: PATTERNITY, London, 2011

Page 34 bottom left, Blind Spots, Photography: PATTERNITY, London, 2011

Page 34 bottom right, Urban Zebra, Photography: PATTERNITY, Sydney, 2011

Page 35 top left, Scribbled Twigs, Photography: PATTERNITY, Hyde Park, London, 2014

Page 35 top right, City Drapes, Photography: PATTERNITY, Hong Kong, 2011

Page 35 bottom left, Holey Façade, Photography: Paul Clemence, Miami, 2014

Page 35 bottom right, Iron Angles, Photography: PATTERNITY, London, 2010

Page 36 top, Wire Waves, Photography: PATTERNITY, London Underground, 2010

Page 36 bottom, Sky Grids, Photography: PATTERNITY, London Bridge, 2014

Page 37 top, Supermarket Stack, Photography: Teddy Cohen, Tel Aviv, Israel, 2014

Page 37 bottom left, Checkered Bib, Photography: Tim Page Whitby/Getty Images, London Fashion Week, SS15, Top: Holly Fulton

Page 37 bottom right, Mono Tiles, Photography: Lukasz Wisniewski/Getty Images

Page 38 top, Totem Tower, Photography: PATTERNITY, Barbican, London, 2014

Page 38 bottom, Satellite Sparkles, Image: NASA Earth Observatory by Jesse Allen and Robert Simmon, Visible infrared imaging radiometer suite and MODIS, 2012

Page 39 top, Streetstyle Stance, Photography: Lyndon Fawcett-Fright, New York, SS14

Page 39 bottom left, Diatom, Image courtesy of ZEISS Microscopy, ZEISS scanning electron microscope

Page 39 bottom right, Drain Circle, Photography: PATTERNITY, Queen Elizabeth Olympic Park, London, 2012

Page 40 top left, Brick Bundle, Photography: PATTERNITY, London, 2014

Page 40 top right, Tyre Tetris, Photography: PATTERNITY, London, 2014

Page 40 bottom left, Seat Repeat, Photography: PATTERNITY, Australia, 2011

Page 40 bottom right, Tidal Jack Stack, Photography: PATTERNITY, Corsica, 2013

Page 41 top left, Tarmac Wrinkles, Photography: PATTERNITY, London, 2010

Page 41 top right, Paint Peels, Photography: PATTERNITY, Australia, 2011

Page 41 bottom left, Broken Links, Photography: Piotr Niepsuj, Berlin

Page 41 bottom right, Crate Collection, Photography: PATTERNITY, New York, 2011

Page 42 top, Stripe Strut, Photography: Gamma Rapho/Getty Images, New York Fashion Week, SS13, Dress: Marc Jacobs

Page 42 bottom, Shadow Shutter, Photography: PATTERNITY, London, 2014

Page 42 middle, Hair Lines, Photography: Teddy Cohen, Tel Aviv, Israel, 2014

Page 43 top left, Frosted Web, Photography: Eye On/Getty Images

Page 43 top right, Window Smash, Photography: PATTERNITY, London, 2014

Page 43 bottom, Bag Lady, Photography: Lyndon Fawcett-Fright, London Fashion Week, 2012

Page 44 top left, Light Strips, Photography: PATTERNITY, London, 2014

Page 44 top right, Grate Grid, Photography: PATTERNITY, New York, 2010

Page 44 bottom left, Plastic Stack, Photography: Jamie Freeth, London, 2014

Page 44 bottom right, Wire Scribble, Photography: PATTERNITY, London, 2014

Page 44 bottom, Shadow Spotting, Photography: PATTERNITY, Anzac Bridge, Sydney, 2014

Page 45, Triangle Tower, Photography: PATTERNITY, Murray Building, Hong Kong, 2011

Pages 46–7, Balcony Bends, Photography: Kane Hulse, Cuba, 2014

Page 48, Step and Repeat, Photography: PATTERNITY, with thanks to the AELTC, Wimbledon AELTC, London, 2015

Page 49, Verdant Verticals, Photography: Gustavo Zylbersztajn, 'Believe The Stripe' for *How To Spend It*, 2013, Model: Fabiana Mayer Ihan @ Way Model, Styling: Damian Foxe

Page 51 top left, Stripe Tease, Photography: Willem Jaspert, 'Fix Up Look Sharp' *B Magazine*, AW11, Model: Aleksandra R @ L.A. Models, Styling: Sam Ranger

Page 51 top right, Ascending Angles, Photography: PATTERNITY, Sydney Opera House, 2011

Page 51 middle left, Bridge Bars, Photography: PATTERNITY, Brazil, 2014

Page 51 middle right, Multi-storey Stripe, Photography: PATTERNITY, Hong Kong, 2011

Page 51 bottom left, Sun Stacks, Photography: PATTERNITY, Croatia, 2011

Page 51 bottom right, Line Order, Photography: Three Lions/Getty Images, Federal District, Mexico City

Page 52, Lane Lines, Photography: Rory van Millingen, London, 2012

Page 53 top left, Stripe Stretch, Photography: John Fort, 2013

Page 53 top right, Pipe Corner, Photography: Rory van Millingen, Beijing, China

Page 53 middle left, Shifting Shadows, Photography: PATTERNITY, Lanzarote, 2014

Page 53 middle right, Comb Teeth, Photography: Neil Watson, 2013

Page 53 bottom left, Stripe in One, Photography: Michael Bodiam, 'Stripes and Dots' Series, 2012, Set Design: Sarah Parker

Page 53 bottom right, Palm Pleats, Photography: PATTERNITY, Ibiza, 2014

Page 54, Lighthouse Levels, Photography: Ed Gilligan, Dungeness, England, 2014

Page 55, Leggy Lines, Photography: Georges Antoni @ The Artist Group, 'SHIM', 2010, Model: Deborah Dunsford

Page 56, PATTERN. CONFLICT. UNITY film, PATTERNITY ∞ IWM, Fleet of Dazzle Range, 2014, Film: Lily Silverton, Model: Georgia Frost, Styling: Julia Brenard, Creative Direction: PATTERNITY

Page 57, Fleet of Dazzle Collection, Photography: PATTERNITY ∞ IWM, Fleet of Dazzle Range, 2014, Creative Direction: PATTERNITY

Pages 58–9 Library Portal, Photography: Nicolas Stjernstrøm Nielsen, Phillips Exeter Academy Library, New Hampshire, USA, 2013

Page 60, Concrete Circles, Photography: PATTERNITY, London, 2012

Page 61, Ring of beauty, Photography: Straulino, Personal project, 2013, Model: J.J @ M4Models.de

Page 62, Everyday Excellence Film, Film: PATTERNITY ∞ COS, 2013, Photography: Neil Watson, Editor: Loren Filis, Creative Direction: PATTERNITY, Fashion: COS Clothing AW13

Page 63, Everyday Excellence Installation, PATTERNITY ∞ COS, 2013, Photography: Neil Watson, Creative Direction: PATTERNITY, Fashion: COS Clothing AW13

Page 65 top left, Hole Style, Photography: PATTERNITY, New York, 2010

Page 65 top right, Shadow Hoops, Photography: Joseph Gibson, Doboj, Bosnia, 2009

Page 65 middle left, Round Reflection, Photography: Helena Anderson, glass on paper

Page 65 middle right, Sun Drain, Photography: PATTERNITY, New York, 2010

Page 65 bottom left, Lobe Loop, Original Silver Earring, COOPS London

Page 65 bottom right, Curve and Curl, Photography: Thomas Brown, 'Constructivist Perfume', Set Design: Storey Studio, 2014

Page 66, Office Spots, Photography: PATTERNITY, Hong Kong, 2011

Page 67, Holes and Corners, Photography: Sarah Piantadosi, Conscious Cloth Lookbook, AW13, Model: Kriss Barupa @ IMG, Styling: Ellie Grace Cumming @ Streeters, Creative Direction: PATTERNITY

Page 68, Black Spot, Photography: Amy Gwatkin, *Dazed Digital* Central St Martins MA 2012 Exclusive, Model: Vanusa @ FM London, Styling: Nelma Lakonji

Page 69 top left, Dalmatian Duo, Photography: Scott Trindle, *i-D* Pre Fall 2013 Street Issue, 2013, Models: Cameron Manocheo @ Next Management and Michael Knowles @ FM London, Styling: Elgar Johnson

Page 69 top right, Parasol Pipes, Photography: PATTERNITY, Nigeria, 2012

Page 69 middle left, Cup Crowd, Photography: PATTERNITY, 2015

Page 69 middle right, Satellite Spots, Photography: PATTERNITY, Nigeria, 2012

Page 69 bottom left, Seat Circles, Photography: PATTERNITY, Ibiza, 2010

Page 69 bottom right, Drainage Dots, Photography: PATTERNITY, San Francisco, 2014

Page 70, Pattern Pioneers Film, Film: PATTERNITY ∞ Clarks Originals, 2014, DOP: Loren Filis, Creative Direction: PATTERNITY, Editor: Sapphire Goss, Sound Design: Jon Dix

Page 71, Shoe Shapes, Footwear: PATTERNITY ∞ Clarks Originals, 2015

Pages 72–3, Check and Step, Photography: PATTERNITY, London, 2015

Page 74, Warped Wire, Photography: Teddy Cohen, Tel Aviv, Israel, 2014

Page 75, Net Wrap, Photography: Niklas Hoejlund, 2011, Model: Anna Trosko @ 2pm Mgmt Aps

Page 77 top left, Checker Out, Photography: Julia Kennedy, *Clash*, AW14, Model: Jenna Roberts @ Select, Styling: Lola Chatterton

Page 77 top right, Grey Grids, Photography: PATTERNITY, Nigeria, 2011

Page 77 middle left, Square Squared, Furniture: DARKROOM, Tiler Cube Table, 2014

Page 77 middle right, Shadow Corner, Photography: Cyan Jordan, Nottingham, England, 2013

Page 77 bottom left, Tilted Tiles, Giles Miller Studio, Cast Metal Tiles

Page 77 bottom right, Grid Glasses, Photography: Karl Donovan, LARKE X DARKROOM, 2014, Styling: Rhonda Drakeford,

Page 78, Bending Bin, Photography: PATTERNITY, Croatia, 2011

Page 79, Lattice Legs, Photography: Jamie Morgan, *Le Monde Tuxedo*, 2013, Model: Valerija Kelava @ Oui Management, Styling: Tom Van Dorpe

Page 80, Balcony Bars, Thumbnail: PATTERNITY ∞ Plastic Horse, City Shapes, Photography: PATTERNITY, Animation: Plastic Horse, Sound: Plastic Horse, London, 2012

Page 81, Venting System, Still: PATTERNITY ∞ Plastic Horse, City Shapes, Photography: PATTERNITY, Animation: Plastic Horse, Sound: Plastic Horse, London, 2012

Page 82, Grid Disguise, Photography: Marlen Keller, *Hunter*, 2014, Model: Charles Markham @ Premier Model Management, Styling: Zuza Stepien

Page 83 top left, Catwalk Cut Out, Photography: Pascal Le Segretain/Getty Images, Paris Fashion Week, SS15, Fashion: Balmain

Page 83 top right, Cyan City, Photography: PATTERNITY, London, 2011

Page 83 middle left, Crossing Clouds, Photography: Agustina Prado Vecchi, New York, 2014

Page 83 middle right, Puffy Pouches, Photography: Catherine Losing, *Cherry Bombe*, 2014, Styling: Iain Graham

Page 83 bottom left, Seat Layer, Photography: PATTERNITY, Edinburgh, 2014

Page 83 bottom right, Solar Panel Pile, Photography: PATTERNITY, Goa, India, 2013

Pages 84–5, Zig-Zag Zone, Photography: PATTERNITY, Kerala, India, 2014

Page 86, Angling Up, Photography: Robert Low, Luxor Hotel, Las Vegas, 2012 www.robertlowstudio.com

Page 87, Neck Steps, Photography: Neil Bedford, *Metal*, 2013, Model: Harry Pulley, Daniel Stowe, Ilan Raes @ Elite Models, Styling: Santi Rodriguez

Page 89 top left, Cheese Wedge, Photography: Paul Taylor/Getty Images

Page 89 top right, Wrapped Railings, Photography: Tom Hobbs, Bristol, England, 2011

Page 89 middle left, Boat Point, Photography: Teddy Cohen, Tel Aviv, Israel, 2014

Page 89 middle right, Tarmac Triangles, Photography: PATTERNITY, Milan, Italy, 2014

Page 89 bottom left, Concrete Cuts, Photography: PATTERNITY, Hong Kong, 2011

Page 89 bottom right, Pyramid Peaks, Photography: Jerzy Bereszko, Giza, Egypt, 2008

Page 90, Marquetry Making, Toby Winteringham Furniture, Photography: Nick Downey, 2013

Page 91, Slicing Shifts, Furniture: PATTERNITY ∞ Toby Winteringham, 'Shift Table', 2011, Mixed Veneer Marquetry

Page 92, Angle Pose, Photography: Andrew Yee, *Syntax Edition #4*, 2010, Styling: Juhee C

Page 93 top left, Jagged Jacket, Photography: Willem Jaspert, Martina Spetlova Lookbook, SS14, Model: Kia Low @ Next Model Management, Styling: Elle Korhaliller

Page 93 top right, Zip Up, Photography: PATTERNITY, 2015

Page 93 middle left, Chevron Shadows, Photography: PATTERNITY, Sydney, 2010

Page 93 middle right, Tacking Tiles, Photography: PATTERNITY, Hong Kong, 2011

Page 93 bottom left, Bridge Bend, Photography: PATTERNITY, Maria Pia Bridge, Portugal, 2012

Page 93 bottom right, Two Tone Tablet, Bethan Gray 'Alice', Photography: Julian Abrams

Page 94, Car Park Crosses, Photography: PATTERNITY, Hong Kong, 2011

Page 95, Facet Jacket, Photography: Brendan Freeman, *Volt*, AW12, Model: Matthew Bell @ Elite Models

Page 96, Conscious Pattern Film, PATTERNITY ∞ Chinti + Parker, 'Conscious Pattern' Film, 2013, Film: Zoe Hitchen, Model: Kriss Barupa @ IMG, Styling: Ellie Grace Cumming @ Streeters, Set Design: PATTERNITY

Page 97, Triangle Kimono, Photography by Sarah Piantadosi, Conscious Cloth Collection, AW13, Model: Kriss Barupa @ IMG, Styling: Ellie Grace Cumming @ Streeters, Creative Direction: PATTERNITY, 2013

Pages 98–9, Viewpoint, Photography: Neil Watson, Barbican, London

Page 102, Blind Beams, Photography: PATTERNITY, London, 2010

Page 103, Passing Phase, Furniture: PATTERNITY ∞ Toby Winteringham, 2011, Hand Cut Marquetry

Page 104, Corner Tile, Photography: PATTERNITY, London, 2013

Page 105, Bricking It, Photography: Neil Watson, Tights: PATTERNITY, 2013

Page 106, Top Tiers, Photography by JTB Photo/Getty, Nyatapola Temple, Nepal

Page 107, Rugged Repeat, Rug: PATTERNITY ∞ Made by Node, 18x18 Node Fairtrade Rugs, 2012, 100 Knot Tibetan Wool

Page 108, Dazzle Ship, Photography: Surgeon Oscar Parkes, courtesy of Imperial War Museums © IWM (SP 706), Dazzle Boat, c.1917

Page 109, Dazzle Pattern, Cushion: PATTERNITY ∞ Imperial War Museums Fleet of Dazzle, 2014

Pages 110–11, Stretched Skin, Photography: Bart Hess, 'Mutants', 2011

Page 112, Top, Speckled Interior, Photography: PATTERNITY, 'Marmoreal' Max Lamb and DZEK at Salone del Mobile, Milan, 2014

Page 112, Bottom, Circle Glass Sculpture, Photography: Ester Segarra, 'Moire Matrix' Shelley James, 2012

Page 113, Top, Tumbling Blocks, Diagram: Public Domain

Page 113, Bottom, Stripe Jelly, Photography: Neil Watson, Bompas & Parr at *PATTERN POWER – Superstripe*, 2013

Page 114 top left, Shipping Shapes, Photography: Nisa and Ulli Maier Photography/Getty Images, Hong Kong Freight Harbour

Page 114 top right, Crossed Contrails, Photography: Andreina Schoeberlein, Gipf-Oberfrick, Switzerland, 2014

Page 114 bottom left, Road Rainbow, Photography: PATTERNITY, London, 2010

Page 114 bottom right, Scattered Signals, Photography: Teddy Cohen, Tel Aviv, Israel, 2014

Page 115 top left, Tile Pile, Photography: PATTERNITY, Lake District, England, 2013

Page 115 top right, Breaking Bark, Photography: PATTERNITY, Melbourne

Page 115 bottom left, Billow Bulge, Photography: PATTERNITY, Goa, India, 2014

Page 115 bottom right, Ice Crumble, Photography: Matt Magill, New York, 2004

Page 116 top, PATTERNITY Kaleidohome, Photography: Say Fromage, PATTERNITY ∞ LDF + Airbnb, 2014

Page 116 middle, Sound Patterns, Photography: Richard Foster, Chladni Plates, 2014

Page 117 top left, Turtle Shell, Photography: iStock by Getty Images

Page 117 top right, Sound Patterns, Photography: Richard Foster, Chladni Plates, 2014

Page 117 middle, Palm Screens, Photography: Gerard Suk, 'We Have No Choice But to Choose', 2008

Page 117 bottom, Toaster Deconstructed, Photography: Daniel Alexander, Thomas Thwaites 'The Toaster Project', 2009

Page 118 top, Children in Springy Thingy, Design: Katie Gaudion, 'Springy Thingy', 2010, Models: Esmé and Amelie

Page 118 bottom, Nepalese Weavers, Photography: Chris Haughton, Made by Node, Kumbeshwar Technical School, Kathmandu, Nepal, 2012

Page 119 top, Phase Bureau, Furniture: PATTERNITY ∞ Toby Winteringham, 2011

Page 119 bottom, William Morris Textile, Textile: William Morris from Morris & Co., Acanthus Tapestry 230272

Page 120 top, Peacock Feather, Photography: Robert Mertens/Getty Images

Page 120 bottom, Data Visualisation T Shirt, PATTERNITY ∞ Environmental Justice Foundation, 2014, Photography: EJF

Page 121 top, Superstripe Loom, Photography: PATTERNITY, Katherine May Weave, 2013

Page 121 bottom, Wildebeest Herd, Photography: Mitsuaki Iwagō/Getty, Blue Wildebeest, Serengeti, Tanzania

Page 122 top, Marble in the Making, Photography: PATTERNITY, Design Museum: 'In the Making', 2014

Page 122 bottom, Plastic Wave, Photography: Jamie Freeth, Cuba

Page 123, Blue Bag Face, Photography: Stuart C. Wilson/Getty Images, Christopher Shannon, AW15, Styling: Isamaya Ffrench

Page 124, Superstripe PATTERNITALK, Photography: PATTERNITY, *PATTERN POWER – Superstripe*, Festival, 2013

Page 125, PATTERNITY Sum Table, PATTERNITY ∞ Toby Winteringham, Monochrome Marquetry Table, 2013

Pages 126–7, Spiral Rounds, Photography: PATTERNITY, 2013, Katie Gaudion, 'Springy Thingy'

Page 128, When Stripes Collide, Thumbnail, 'When Stripes Collide' PATTERNITY ∞ Lily Silverton, Film: Lily Silverton, Model: Terri McGlone @ Storm, Editor: Eddie Wrey, Stylist: Tui Lin, 2013

Page 129, When Stripes Collide, Stills, 'When Stripes Collide' PATTERNITY ∞ Lily Silverton, Film: Lily Silverton, Model: Terri McGlone @ Storm, Editor: Eddie Wrey, Stylist: Tui Lin, 2013

Page 130, Wondrous Weavers, Thumbnail, Film: Omar O'sullivan and Chris Haughton, Kumbeshwar Technical School, Kathmandu, Nepal, 2012

Page 131, PATTERNITY Sun Stripe Rug, Photography: Neil Watson, Set Design: Katie Fotis

Pages 132–3, Geometric Set, Photography and Set Design: Storey Studio, *The Fractured and The Feline*, Exhibition, Quentin Jones and Robert Storey, 2014

Page 134, Theobromine Molecule, Diagram: PATTERNITY

Page 135, PATTERNITY Structure of Chocolate Installation, Photography: Kate Jackling, PATTERNITY ∞ Pierre Marcolini for *Wallpaper* Handmade 2014*, Manufacture: Toby Winteringham, Set Design: Katie Fotis

Pages 136–7, PATTERNITY Ceramics, Photography: Neil Watson, PATTERNITY ∞ Richard Brendon, 'Warp + Reason Tea Set', 2013

Page 138, PATTERNITY Window Installation, Photography: Neil Watson, Selfridges: 'Bright Young Things', Set Design: PATTERNITY, Oxford Street, London, 2011

Page 139, PATTERNITY Tights, Photography: Neil Watson, Tights: PATTERNITY, 'Block Out', 'Trademark' and 'Totem' tights, 2011

Pages 140–1, PATTERNITY Kaleidohome, Photography: Ed Gilligan, PATTERNITY ∞ LDF + Airbnb, 'Kaleidohome', Trafalgar Square, London, 2014

218

Pages 144–5, DPS, Bouquet Agate, Photography: D. R. 'Matt' Dillon, Bouquet Agate, Texas, USA, 2010

Page 146, Paint Power, Photography: Thomas Brown, '(x-a)2+(y-b)2=r2 Circles', 2012, Set Design: Lightning + Kinglyface

Page 147, Floral Flash, Photography: Viviane Sassen, *Dazed & Confused,* 2011, Model: Lisanne de Jong @ Ulla Models, Styling: Katie Shillingford

Page 148, Creature Curls, Photography: Tim Flach, 'More than Human', 2012, Centipedes

Page 149, Body Bind, Photography: Gamma Rapho/Getty Images, Paris Haute Couture Week, AW11

Page 150 top, Winding River, Photography: Paul Kiler, USA, 2014

Page 150 bottom, Hadron Collider, Photography: CERN, Large Hadron Collider

Page 151 top, Branching Trees, Photography: PATTERNITY, London, 2012

Page 151 bottom left, Brain Scan, Imaging: Sovereign, ISM/Science Photo Library, Healthy MRI Scan

Page 151 bottom right, Purple Cabbage, Photography: PATTERNITY, Purple Cabbage cross section, 2015

Page 152 top left, Fungus Fans, Photography: Kalin Hart Talbott, Carmel Beach, California, 2014

Page 152 top right, Sand Contours, Photography: Toby Winteringham, Norfolk, England, 2010

Page 152 bottom left, Tripe Ripples, Photography: Neil Watson, PATTERNITY for *Wolf*, 2012

Page 152 bottom right, Pollen Pops, Photography: PATTERNITY, Botanical Gardens, Rio De Janeiro, Brazil, 2014

Page 153 top left, Lichen Landscape, Photography: PATTERNITY, Ilha Grande, Brazil, 2014

Page 153 top right, Arid and Aerial, Photography: Paul Kiler, Arizona, USA, 2013

Page 153 bottom left, Woven Layers, Photography: PATTERNITY, Columbia, 2010

Page 153 bottom right, Tangled Treads, Photography: PATTERNITY, Lanzarote, 2014

Page 154 top, Romanesco Broccoli, Photography: PATTERNITY, Romanesco Broccoli, 2015

Page 154 bottom, Giants Causeway, Photography: Deirdre Gregg, www.deirdregregg.com, 2010

Page 155 top, Golden Section, Diagram: Public Domain

Page 155 middle, Ammonite, Photography: De Agostini/Getty

Page 155 bottom, Spiral Galaxy, Imaging by NASA, ESA, S. Beckwith (STScI), & the Hubble Heritage Team (STScI/AURA), Whirlpool Galaxy Hubble ACS visible image of M51, Hubble telescope, 2011

Page 156 top, Human Proportions, diagram courtesy of Neufert-Stiftung, Germany, Bauentwurfslehre, 1936

Page 156 bottom, Divine Proportions, Film: Benjamin Seroussi, 'Divine Proportions', 2012, Model: Lorelle Crawford @ Tamblyn Modelling

Page 157 top, Green Palm Pleats, Photography: PATTERNITY, Brazil, 2014

Page 157 bottom, Commuter Chaos, Photography: China Foto Press/Getty Images, Traffic in Xi An, China

Page 158 top left, Rugged Rocks, Photography: Michael Chichi, Oregon, 2011

Page 158 top right, Iris Crater, Photography: Suren Manvelyan, 'Your Beautiful Eyes'

Page 158 bottom left, Mars View, Photography: NASA/JPL/UA, Victoria Crater' at Meridiani Planum, Mars, 2006 NASA Mars Reconnaissance Orbiter

Page 158 bottom right, Jaguar Blotches, Photography: S B Nace/Getty Images

Page 159 top left, Orchid Butterfly, Photography: Neil Watson, 2013

Page 159 top right, Head on View, Photography: Peter Dazeley/Getty Images, Brain Scan

Page 159 bottom left, Penguin Pair, Photography: Paul Mannix, Boulders Beach, South Africa, 2007

Page 159 bottom right, Rorschach Form, Photography: Scott Baumann, Rorschach, 2008, Ink and Paper

Page 160 top, Body Sculpture, Photography: AFP/Getty Images, Fashion: Iris Van Herpen, Paris Haute Couture Week, AW11

Page 160 bottom, Ice Layers, Photography: Lida Marinkova, Iceland, 2013

Page 161 top, Shark Skin, Photography: Sharklet Technologies, Electron Micrograph

Page 161 middle, Tech Surface, Photography: Sharklet Technologies

Page 161 bottom, Circle Farms, Photography: Paul Kiler, USA, 2013

Page 162 top, César Manrique Sculpture, Photography: PATTERNITY, César Manrique Foundation, Lanzarote, 2014

Page 162 bottom, Navajo Indian wedding basket, Photography: Universal Images Group/Getty Images, Navajo Indian Reservation, Arizona

Page 163 top, Blue PATTERNITILE, Photography: PATTERNITY, Nigeria, Hong Kong, London

Page 163 bottom, Olafur Eliasson Sculpture, Photography: PATTERNITY, Inhotim Contemporary Art Museum, Brazil, 2014

Pages 164–5, Road Shapes, Photography: Ivan Shaw, Perth, Australia, 2012

Page 166, Rusty Rivers, Photography: Bernhard Edmaier, Laguna Roja, Chile, 2012

Page 167, Hair Slithers, Photography: Georges Antoni @ The Artist Group, *Oyster*, 2011, Model: Phoebe Griffiths @ Chic Models

Page 168, Dune Movement, Photography: Jeremy Woodhouse/Getty Images, Merzouga, Morocco

Page 169, Sleek Shoulder Shine, Photography: SCANDEBERGS, 'Hair', 2013, Model: Chiara Riva

Page 170, Bubble Universe, Photography: Neil Watson, 2006

Page 171 top left, Hex-Ray Vision, Photography: firstVIEW, Paris Fashion Week, SS10, Sunglasses: Hussein Chalayan

Page 173 top right, Sud Cells, Photography: Dirk Wiersma, 'Soap Bubbles', 2013

Page 173 middle left, Honeycomb Hanging, Photography: Gavin Mackintosh, Quince Honey Farm, Devon, 2011

Page 173 middle right, Hexadome, Photography: Jamie Freeth, The Eden Project, Cornwall, 2014

Page 173 bottom left, Bolted Brass, Photography: PATTERNITY, 2015

Page 173 bottom right, Scale Structure Skin, Photography: Steven Snodgrass, albino boa constrictor, 2009

Page 174, Volcanic Shore, Photography: PATTERNITY, El Golfo, Lanzarote, 2014

Page 175, Sulphur Explorer, Photography: Willem Jaspert, Iceland, 2007

Page 176, Moss Mounds, Photography: Katarzyna Pilipionek, Lava Field, Iceland, 2013

Page 177, Fashion Fuzz, Photography: Victor Virgile/Getty Images, Paris Fashion Week, Celine, AW13

Page 178, Phytoplankton Swirl, Photography: NASA Goddard Space Flight Center/USGS, Phytoplankton swirl in dark water, Gotland, Swedish island in the Baltic Sea, 2005, Landsat 7

Page 179, Space Suit, Photography: Andrew Vowles, PATTERNITY ∞ Berthold, SS13, Model: Miles Hurley @ Next Models, Styling: John Colver

Page 180 top left, Cracked Up, Photograph: Getty Images, New York Fashion Week, AW14, Proenza Schouler AW14

Page 181 top right, Geo Giraffe, Photography: Teddy Cohen, Ramat Gan, Israel, 2014

Page 181 middle left, Ice Path, Photography: Bernhard Edmaier, Disco Bay, Greenland

Page 181 middle right, Crackle Glaze, Photography: Heritage Images/Getty Images, Southern Song Dynasty, China, 13th Century

Page 181 bottom left, Green Network, Photography: PATTERNITY, Savoy cabbage, 2015

Page 181 bottom right, Crazed Paving, Photography: PATTERNITY, Australia, 2011

Page 182, Rainbow Road, Photography: Piers Rutterford, London, 2007

Page 183, Technicolour Tresses, Photography: Mark Pillai, *Dazed & Confused,* 2009, Model: Anastasia Kuznetsova @ Next Models, Styling: Katie Shillingford

Page 184, Water Wiggle, Photography: PATTERNITY, Museo César Manrique, Lanzarote, 2014

Page 185, Holographic Walk, Photography: ImaxTree, Paris Fashion Week, AW12

Page 187 top left, Scribble Stance, Photography: Simon Burstall, *Hunger #7*, 2014, Model: Grace Bol @ Storm, Styling: Kim Howells

Page 187 top right, Whale Wave, Photography: Tom Sewell, Pilot Whale, Tenerife, 2014

Page 187 middle left, Car Crunch, Photography: Piotr Niepsuj, Italy, 2014

Page 187 middle right, Window Waves, Photography: PATTERNITY, Australia, 2011

Page 187 bottom left, Water Planes, Photography: Lyndon Fawcett-Fright, Margate, England, 2012

Page 187 bottom right, Indigo Folds, Photography: Fran Buss, Screen print, 2014

Page 188, Painted Swirl, Photography: Neil Watson, paint on paper, 2010

Page 189, Shrouded Smoke, Photography: Mel Bles, 2009, Styling: Stevie Westgarth

Page 190, Meat Marble, Photography: Neil Watson, PATTERNITY for *Wolf*, 2012

Page 191, Material Mash Up, Photography by Kate Jackling, 'Babinets Playground', 2014, Set Design: Lightning + Kinglyface

Pages 192–3, Crack Down, Photography: PATTERNITY, USA, 2014

Page 195 top left, Tree Top, Photography: Getty Images, New York Fashion Week, SS14, Proenza Schouler AW14

Page 195 top right, Energy Forks, Photography: Alan Osterholtz, New Mexico, USA, 2014

Page 195 middle left, Breathing Branches, Photography: CNRI/Science Photo Library, Lung Bronchioles, X-Ray

Page 195 middle right, Meandering Mountains, Photography: Bernhard Edmaier, Death Valley, USA

Page 195 bottom left, Hand Holds, Photography: SCANDEBERGS, Hands, 2014, Model: Nicola Baratto, Marta Modena, Fanny Muggiani

Page 165 bottom right, Pastel Fractals, Photography: PATTERNITY, Lincolnshire, England, 2013

Page 196, Jelly Domes, Photograph: Lionel Cironneau/Associated Press, Moon Jellyfish, Oceanographic Museum of Monaco, 2010

Page 197, Draped in Dots, Photography: Paul Maffi, *Transmission*, AW13, Model: Samantha Gradoville @ IMG

Page 199 top left, Flecked Flair, Photography: Osma Harvilahti, Satu Maaranen Lookbook, 2014, Fashion: Satu Maaranen

Page 199 top right, Crowded Craniums, Photography: Stockbyte/Getty Images, 1940s

Page 199 middle left, Gestalt Floor, Photography: PATTERNITY, Croatia, 2014

Page 199 middle right, Pony Patches, Photography: Bob Langrish/Getty Images, Appaloosa Horse

Page 199 bottom left, Serving Splatter, Photography: Labour and Wait

Page 199 bottom right, Blotched Beans, Photography: Trade Winds Fruit www.tradewindsfruit.com, Orca Beans

Page 200, Flamingo Flecks, Photograph: Michael Poliza, Lake Bogoria, Kenya, 2011

Page 201, Full On Fur, Photography: Brendan Freeman, *USED*, 2013, Model: Diana Farkhullina @ Premier Model Management, Styling: Kimi O'Neill

Pages 206–7, DPS, Curtain Call, Photography: Tim Gutt, *POP*, 2009, Set Design: Shona Heath

Page 208, Harlequin Shrimp, Photography by Luiz A. Rocha/Shutterstock , Bali, Indonesia

p.209, Camo Couture, Photography by Ben Weller, *W Magazine*, 2013, Model: Maryna Linchuk @ DNA, Styling: Patrick Mackie

Page 210, Palm Springs, Photography by Sofie Hermans, Barcelona, 2012

Page 211, Fan Flare, Photography by Ahmet Unver, *L'Officiel Turkey*, 2014, Model: Claudia Anticevic @ Model Scouting Office, Styling: Ayça Elkap

Page 212, Wonderwave, Photography: PATTERNITY, Ihla Grande, Brazil, 2014

Page 213, Drape Drench, Photography: Patric Shaw, 2002, Model: Unknown, Crêpe Voile

Page 224, PATTERNITY cofounders, Left, Anna Murray, Right, Grace Winteringham, Karoliina Bärlund, 2013

INDEX

Page numbers in *italic* refer to images

A

Abstract Expressionism 151
Acne Studios 9
Adobe 113
Airbnb 116
Alexander, Christopher 161
Alsop, Louise 77
Anders, William 202
Angle Pose 92
Angling Up 86
angular patterns 180
animation, *City Shapes* 80, *80–1*
Antoni, Georges *20–1, 55, 167*
Apple 113
Archimedes 203
Arid and Aerial *153*
Art Deco 120
Ascending Angles *51*
Attenborough, David 116
Auerbach, Tauba 30
Aurelius, Marcus 123, 147, 197

B

Balcony Bends *46–7*
Ball, Philip 14, 155, 156
Balmain 83
Banks, Sir Joseph *154–5*
Barber, Edward 117
Bateson, Gregory 31, 32, 33, 42, 161
Bedford, Neil 87
Beijing National Stadium 160
Bell, Vanessa 112
Bending Bin *78*
Benyus, Janine 160
benzene 172
Berlin, Isaiah 30
Berners-Lee, Tim 203
Berthold *179*
Beyond Retro *201*
Bi Sheng 38
Billow Bulge *115*
biomimicry 160, 161
Biophilia Live 116
Björk 116
Black Spot *68*
Blake, William 37
Bles, Mel *189*
Blind Beams *102*
Blind Spots *34*
blogs 38–9
Bloomsbury Group 112
Blotched Beans *199*
blotches 198
Blue Bag Face *123*
Blumarine *183*
Boat Point *89*

Body Bind *149*
Bolted Brass *173*
Bompas, Sam 113
Bompas & Parr 113, *113*
Bono, Edward de 112
Bor, Daniel 160
Bouquet Agate *144–5*
branches 194
Breaking Bark *115*
Breathing Branches *195*
Brendon, Richard 121, *136–7*
Brick Bundle *40*
Bricking It *105*
Bridge Bars *51*
Bridge Bend *93*
Broken Links *41*
Brown, Thomas *146*
Browne, Sir Thomas 150, 177
Bubble Universe *170*
bubbles 30, *31*
Buckminster Fuller, R. 162
Buddha, Gautama 36, 105
Buddhism 64
Burke, Edmund 25

C

Cable Spray *28*
Camo Couture *209*
camouflage 56, *56–7*
Capra, Fritjof 33, 161, 179
Car Crunch *187*
Car Park Crosses *94*
carbon nanotubes (CNT) 172
Catwalk Cut Out *83*
Céline 42, *177*
cells 172
ceramics 121
Chalayan, Hussein *173, 185*
Chambers, Tony 112
Chanel 42
Check and Step *72–3*
Checker Out *77*
Cheese Wedge *89*
Chevron Shadows *93*
China 90, 180
Chinti and Parker 25, 67, 96, *96–7*, 120–1
chocolate 134
Christianity 64
Cicero, Marcus Tullius 87
circles 64
Cironneau, Lionel *196*
City Drapes *35*
City Shapes 80, *80–1*
Clapiers, Luc de 109
Clark, Nathan 70
Clarks Originals 70, *70–1*
clouds 31, *31, 36,* 154
Cohen, Teddy 74

coincidence 159
collaboration 112–41
Columbus, Christopher 150, 202
Comb Teeth *53*
Concrete Circles *60*
Concrete Cuts *89*
connectivity 142–201
Conscious Cloth *25*
'Conscious Cloth Meets Conscious
  Pattern' 96, *96–7*
Conscious Pattern 96, *96*
consumption 114, 117–18
contours 186
COOPS 65
Copernicus 203
Corner Tile *104*
COS 62, *62–3*
cosmological imagery 64, 202–3
Coulomb, Nicolas 11
Crack Down *192–3*
Cracked Up *181*
Crackle Glaze *181*
Crackle Scape *34*
cracks 180
Crate Collection *41*
Crazed Paving *181*
Creased Collection *11*
creases 186
Creature Curls *148*
Crossed Contrails *114*
Crossing Clouds *83*
Crowded Craniums *199*
Csikszentmihalyi, Mihaly 202
cubes 76
Cup Crowd *69*
Curie, Marie 203
Curtain Call *206–7*
Curve and Curl *65*
curves 64
Cyan City *83*

D

Dalai Lama 36
Dalí, Salvador 156
Dalmatian Duo *69*
dapples 198
Darwin, Charles 31, 202
David, David 30
Dazzle Pattern *109*
Dazzle Ship *108*
Design Museum, London 117
diamonds 88
Dillon, D. R. 'Matt' *144–5*
Dior 87
Dior Homme *5*
Divine Proportions 156, *156*
Dixon, Tom 15
Dolce & Gabbana *49*
Donne, John 121, 167

Drain, Jim 32
Drainage Dots *69*
Drape Drench *213*
Draped in Dots *197*
Dune Movement *168*

E

Eames, Charles and Ray 150
Earls, Mark 121
Earth 202–3
Edmaier, Bernhard *166*
education edible installation 134, *134–5*
Egyptians, Ancient 162
Einstein, Albert 29
Eliasson, Olafur 163
Energy Forks *195*
The Environmental Justice Foundation
  120, 121
Eriksen, Jens 88
ethical knitwear 96, *96–7*, 120–1
Exactitudes exhibition (2008) 32
exploration 142–201, 202
'Exposition Internationale des Arts
  Décoratifs et Industriels Modernes'
  (1925) 120

F

Facet Jacket *95*
facets 180
fair trade 130
Fan Flare *211*
Fashion Fuzz *177*
Fenton, Nick 116
Ffrench, Isamaya *123*
Fibonacci 155, 203
films
  Biophilia Live 116
  Conscious Pattern 96, *96*
  Divine Proportions 156, *156*
  Pattern.Conflict.Unity 56, *56*
  Pattern Pioneers 70, *70*
  Powers of Ten 150
  Samsara 117
  When Stripes Collide 128, *128–9*
Flach, Tim *148*
Flamingo Flecks *200*
Flecked Flair *199*
flecks 198
Fleet of Dazzle 56, *56–7, 109,* 121
Floral Flash *147*
Forcefield art collective 32
Foster + Partners 42
fractal geometry 154, 194
fractography 180
The Fractured and the Feline *132–3*
Franklin, Benjamin 203
Freeman, Brendan *95, 201*
Fricke, Ron 117

Frize, Bernard 8
Froebel, Friedrich 118
Full on Fur 201
Fulton, Holly 14, 36–7, 37
Fungus Fans 152
furniture
 Phase Bureau 103, 119, 119
 Shift Table 90–1, 119
 Sum Marquetry Table 124, 124–5

G

Gabaldon, Diana 157, 191
Galilei, Galileo 30–1, 203
Gamma Rapho 149
Gaudion, Katie 118, 118, 126–7, 128
Geo Giraffe 181
Geometric Set 132–3
geometry 30–1, 32
Gestalt Floor 199
Gevinson, Tavi 39
Gilligan, Ed 54, 140–1
Goethe, Johann Wolfgang von 156
Gold Drapes 7
Golden Ratio 155, 156–7, 156
Grant, Evan 116
Granta 118
Gray, Kevin Francis 7
Greeks, Ancient 30, 64
Green Network 181
Grey Grids 77
Grid Disguise 82
Grid Glasses 77
grids 76
Griffin, Michael 187
Gucci 147
Gursky, Andreas 117
Gutt, Tim 206–7
Gwatkin, Amy 29, 68
Gyatso, Tenzin 36

H

Hair Slithers 167
Hand Holds 195
Harlequin Shrimp 208
Hartley, Nik 9
Head on View 159
Heffernan, Margaret 204
'Hello, My Name is Paul Smith' exhibition
 (2014) 117
Heraclitus 43
Hermans, Sofie 210
Herpen, Iris van 43, 149, 160, 160
Herzog, Jacques 160
Heskett, Professor John 120
Hess, Bart 110–11, 116
Hex-Ray Vision 173
Hexadome 173
hexagons 172

Hillary, Edmund 150
Hinduism 64
Hitchen, Zoe 96
Hockney, David 160
Hoejlund, Niklas 75
Hole Style 65
holes 64
Holes and Corners 67
Holey Façade 35
Holographic Walk 185
Honeycomb Hangings 173
hoops 64
hosiery 138, 138–9
How It's Made 117
Hugo, Victor 150
Hulse, Kane 46–7
Huxley, Thomas Henry 79

I

IBM 154
Ice Crumble 115
Ice Path 181
ImaxTree 185
Imperial War Museums, London 56, 109,
 121
'In The Making' exhibition (2014) 117
Indigo Folds 187
Industrial Revolution 113
Inhotim Contemporary Art Museum, Brazil
 163
innovation 100–41
inspiration 22–99
interconnectivity 158
internet 38–9
Iris Crater 158
Iron Angles 35

J

Jackling, Kate 191
Jacobs, Marc 42
Jagged Jacket 93
Jaguar Blotches 158
James, Shelley 112
James, William 107, 117, 160, 185
Jaspert, Willem 51, 93, 175
Jeanneret-Gris, Charles-Édouard 120
Jelly Domes 196
Jones, Quentin 132–3
JTB Photo 106
Judd, Donald 42

K

KALEIDOHOME 116, 116, 140–1
Kane, Christopher 160
Karlsson, Anna-Karin 49
Keller, Marlen 82

Kennedy, Julia 77
Kepler, Johannes 156
Khan, Hazrat Inayat 151
knitwear, ethical 96, 96–7, 120–1
Koch snowflake 31
Kondranina, Yulia 29
Koren, Leonard 5, 37
Kors, Michael 209
Kostadinov, Kiko 52
Kris Van Assche 5
Kuhn, Thomas 123
Kumbeshwar Technical School 130
Kupferberg, Tuli 205
Kurzweil, Ray 43
Kusama, Yayoi 30

L

Lamb, Max 112
Lane Lines 52
Lang, Fritz 14
Large Hadron Collider 150, 150
LARKE X DARKROOM 77
Lattice Legs 79
Lawlor, Derek 189
Le Corbusier 120, 156
Leggy Lines 55
Library Portal 58–9
Lichen Landscape 153
Lighthouse Levels 54
Lightning + Kinglyface 146, 191
Line Lady 27
Line Order 51
lines 50
Lobe Loop 65
London Design Festival (2014) 116
Loos, Adolf 120
Low, Robert 86
LucyAndBart 116

M

Maaranen, Satu 199
Made by Node 107, 130
Maffi, Paul 197
Mandelbrot, Benoît 31, 154
Manrique, César 42, 49, 162, 162
marbles 180
Marcolini, Pierre 134
Mars View 158
Marshall, Hannah 92
Marx, Karl 113
Material Mash Up 191
materials 115
May, Katherine 121
McGilchrist, Iain 33, 55
McLaren, Malcolm 112
McRae, Lucy 116
meander 194
Meandering Mountains 195

Meat Marble 190
Meuron, Pierre de 160
Mies van der Rohe, Ludwig 76
Millingen, Rory van 52
mindfulness 34, 36
Mitchell, Edgar D 202
Miyake, Issey 9, 30, 95
Modernism 76, 112
Mondrian, Piet 76
Mono Man 5
Montessori, Maria 118
Morgan, Jamie 79
Morris, William 22, 119, 119
Moss Mounds 176
Mountain Pleats 10
Muir, John 151, 211
Multi-storey Stripe 51

N

NASA Goddard Space Flight Center/
 USGS 178
Native Americans 162, 162
nature 31, 33, 151–63, 186, 198
Neck Steps 87
Net Wrap 75
nets 76
Neufert, Ernst 156
Nietzsche, Friedrich 155
Nike 42
'non-places' 35, 80

O

Oceanographic Museum of Monaco 196
Office Spots 66
Orchid Butterfly 159
Osgerby, Jay 117
Osondu, E C 118

P

Paint Peels 41
Paint Power 146
Painted Swirl 188
Palahniuk, Chuck 44, 67
Palm Pleats 53
Palm Springs 210
Palm Streamers 6
Parasol Pipes 69
Parkes, Surgeon Oscar 108
Parr, Henry 113
Passing Phase 103
Pastel Fractals 195
Pattern.Conflict.Unity 56, 56
Pattern Pioneers 70, 70
PATTERN POWER – Superstripe (2013)
 113, 121, 121, 124, 128, 128–9, 160
PATTERNITALKS 124, 128
PATTERNITRIPS 44, 44, 162

PATTERNITY KALEIDOHOME 116, *116*, 140–1
patterns, definition of 16–17
Penguin Pair *159*
Penrose Triangle *113*
Phase Bureau *103*, 119, *119*
Phoenicians 38
Phytoplankton Swirl *178*
Piantadosi, Sarah *25*, *67*
Pilipionek, Katarzyna *176*
Pillai, Mark *5*, *183*
Pipe Corner *53*
Plastic Horse 80
Plato 30, 95
Plotinus 103, 155
Poliza, Michael *200*
Pollen Pops *152*
Pollock, Jackson 151
polygons *172*
Pony Patches *199*
Pope, Alexander 142
Powers of Ten 150
Proenza Schouler *181*, *195*
Proust, Marcel 18
Puffy Pouches *83*
Pugh, Gareth 30
punk movement 112
Pyramid Peaks *89*
pyramids 88

Q
Quarry Block Out *20–1*

R
Rainbow Road *182*
Rectangle Repeat *24*
Reggio, Godfrey 38
Rellik *201*
Renaissance 30–1
repeats 50
Riley, Bridget 36–7
Ring of Beauty *61*
rings 64
ripples 186
Road Rainbow *114*
Road Shapes *164–5*
Rocha, Luiz A. *208*
Romantic poets 31
Rorschach Form *159*
Rory DCS *27*
Round Reflections *65*
Rousse, Georges 113
Rugged Repeat *107*
Rugged Rocks *158*
rugs *107*, 118, 130, *130–1*
Russell, Bertrand 118
Rusty Rivers *166*
Rutterford, Piers *182*

S
sacred geometry *32*
Sagan, Carl 203
Samsara 117
Sand Contours *152*
Sassen, Viviane *147*
Satellite Spots *69*
Scale Structure Skin *173*
SCANDEBERGS *169*
Scattered Signals *114*
scent patterns 33
Schneider, Michael S 32
Schuman, Scott 39
Scribble Stance *187*
Scribbled Twigs *35*
Scutt, Danielle *51*
Seat Circles *69*
Seat Layer *83*
Seat Repeat *40*
Selfridges 138
Sella, Andrea 75
senses 115, 116
Seroussi, Benjamin 156, *156*
Serving Splatter *199*
Shadow Corner *77*
Shadow Hoops *65*
Shadow Steps *34*
Shannon, Christopher *123*
Shaw, Ivan *164–5*
Shaw, Patric *213*
Shift Table *90–1*, 119
Shifting Shadows *53*
Shipping Shapes *114*
shoes 70, *70–1*
Shrouded Smoke *189*
Shutter Chevrons *26*
Silverton, Lily 56, 128
Sleek Shoulder Shine *169*
Smith, Paul 117
Smith, Robert Rowland 15
Smolan, Rick 39
Solar Panel Pile *83*
sound patterns 33
space 202–3
Space Suit *179*
speckles 198
Spetlova, Martina *93*
Spinoza, Baruch 162
Spiral Rounds *126–7*
spots 64
Square Squared *77*
squares 76, 88
stacks 50
stars 30, *30*
Step and Repeat *48*
'step and repeat' repetition 113, *113*
steps 50
Stjernstrøm Nielsen, Nicolas *58–9*
Storey Studio *132–3*
Straulino *61*

Stretched Skin *110–11*
Strickland, Peter 116
Stripe Stretch *53*
Stripe Tease *51*
stripes 50
Stripes in One *53*
'Structure of Chocolate' 134, *134–5*
Sud Cells *173*
Sulphur Explorer *175*
Sum Marquetry Table 124, *124–5*
Sun Drain *65*
Sun Stacks *51*
Superabundant exhibition (2009) 32

T
tables
    Shift Table *90–1*, 119
    Sum Marquetry Table 124, *124–5*
Tacking Tiles *93*
Tangled Treads *153*
Tarmac Triangles *89*
Tarmac Wrinkles *41*
Tassel Triangle *29*
Technicolour Tresses *183*
Technicolour Weave *8*
tesselate *172*
texture 115, 116
theobromine 134, *134*
Thích Nhất Hanh 36, 61
Thomsen, Malene List 68
Thoreau, Henry David 36
Thwaites, Thomas 117, 118
Tidal Jack Stack *40*
Tile Pile *115*
tiles 76
Tilted Tiles *77*
Top Tiers *106*
Tree Top *195*
Trellis Trousers *9*
triangles 88
Trindle, Scott *69*
Tripe Ripples *152*
Turing, Alan 157
Turvey, Joseph *69*
Two Tone Tablet *93*
Tyre Tetris *40*

U
Uniqlo *9*
Unver, Ahmet *211*
Urban Zebra *34*
Uyttenbroek, Ellie 32

V
Vent Lines *4*
Verdant Verticals *49*

Versace 27
Versluis, Ari 32
Viewpoint *98–9*
Volcanic Shore *174*
Volkswagen 42
Vowles, Andrew *179*
Voyager I 150, 203

W
*Wallpaper**
    Design Award (2011) 90, 119
    Handmade (2014) 112, 134
Warp + Reason Ceramics *136–7*
Warped Wire *74*
Water Planes *187*
Water Wiggle *184*
Watson, Neil *98–9*, *105*, *126–7*, *170*, *188*, *190*
waves 186
Wellcome Collection 112
Weller, Ben *209*
Westwood, Vivienne 42, 112
Whale Wave *187*
When Stripes Collide 128, *128–9*
White, Frank 203
Whitehead, Alfred North 120
Wilson, Stuart C *123*
Window Waves *187*
Winteringham, Toby
    Phase Bureau *103*, 119, *119*
    Shift Table 90, *90–1*
    'Structure of Chocolate' 134, *134–5*
    Sum Marquetry Table 124, *124–5*
Wonderwave *212*
Woodhouse, Jeremy *168*
Woolf, Virginia 112
Wordsworth, William 157, 201
Woven Layers *153*
Wrapped Railings *89*

Y
YCN 80
Yee, Andrew *92*

Z
Zeno of Elea 149
Zig-Zag Zone *84–5*
zigzags 88
Zip Up *93*
Zylbersztajn, Gustavo 49

WITH GRATITUDE

'Nothing ever exists entirely alone;
everything is in relation to everything else.'

Gautama Buddha (c.563–483BC)

We would like to express our gratitude to those who have joined us on the exciting journey of making our first book. From the seed of an idea to the final result we can now hold in our hands; it has been quite the adventure.

Firstly our special thanks to our contributing editor Dal Chodha, who has been instrumental in the making of this book. Your expert insight and steadfast guidance has kept us motivated at the times we needed it most.

Our thanks to the team at Conran Octopus: to Joe Cottington, Polly Poulter, Juliette Norsworthy and Jane Ace for their belief and sensitive crafting of our ideas, thoughts and teachings. And to Hellie Ogden at Janklow & Nesbit, who has been there every step of the way. Also, the fresh eyes of those who gave their time and energy to read through early transcripts – Dr Elle Parker, Jessie Brinton, John Ashworth, Philip Ball and Sophie Portas – we are so appreciative.

To our incredible PATTERNITEAM, both past and present, we owe enormous thanks! Firstly to Liv Taylor whose patience, persistence and commitment to research is truly valued. We couldn't have done it without you. To Ben De Silva, Charlotte McConnell, Chris Newlove Horton, Colin Henderson, Didi Wambugu, Gemma Jones, James Payne-Gill, Joseph Gibson, Justyna Michalowska, Laura Shrimpton, Lauren T-Franks, Louisa Ziane, Loren Filis, Lyndon Fawcett-Fright, Lucy Jones, Martin Krause, Molly Mccabe, Neil Watson, Paul Isaac, Rory DCS, Selene Collins, Timothy Anscombe-Bell, all our students and the PATTERN POWER – Superstripe Team and to Will Perrens. Your valuable skills, input and faith in us are bound within these pages.

We have been honoured to work with many inspiring individuals, brands and institutions along the way. Special thanks to Holly Fulton, Robert Rowland Smith, Tom Dixon, Tony Chambers and Amy Heffernan at *Wallpaper**, Airbnb, Apple, Ash and Ella, Assembly London, BAF Graphics, Barbican, Bompas & Parr, Clarks Originals, Chinti + Parker, COS, Darkroom London, Diaggeo, Environmental Justice Foundation, Fred Butler, Getty Images, Google, Guerilla Science, Granta, Imperial War Museums, Jill & Tula, Katharine Hamnett, Lily Silverton, London Design Festival, Made by Node,

Mat Humphrey, Nick Defty, Nike, Plastic Horse, Richard Brendon, Richard Weston, Robert Storey, Shelley James, Supercollider and Zoe Hitchen. You have helped us to implement our ideas and cemented our belief in the positive and unifying power of pattern.

To our parents, for their endless faith and instilling in us the core values that continually drive us forward. Particularly Andy, Judith and the Murray family, Vicki, Toby and the Winteringham family, and to our smorgasbord of wonderful friends especially those who have shown particular support – Alice Gee, Emmie Sharp, Emily Stone, Emily Wassall, Flora Parkinson, FNAF, Gabby Hales, Jambon, Jamie Freeth, Jess Outred, Lionel Skerratt, Lucy Murray, Matt Barnes, Neil Pemberton, Nick Curnow, Nick Griffiths, Robin Mellor, Rob Morrison and Will Griffiths.

To our many sounding boards and supporters along the road: Alex Bec, Alex and Dean, Andrew Scott, Björn Thomas Atterstam, Candice, Curious Minds Club, Darron Cox, Dave Murray, LSBC, Elle Hankinson, Jane Shepherdson, Jeff Gilbert, Linda Hewson, Mary-Alice Stack, Melissa Hemsley, Olivia Triggs, Oliver Vicars-Harris, Pamela Kelly, Pigalle Tavakkoli, Rob, Peter and Lisa at Londonewcastle, Rhona Clews, Rosco, Roxy Houshmand, Sabine Zetteler, Sam Bennett, Sarah Quinn, Stevie Wilde and to Wynne Griffiths and the Griffiths family.

To our network of pattern lovers across the world – without whom none of this would have been possible. To those who have been inspired by our research, attended our many events over the years, bought our products, attended our talks and shared their ideas and research with us. You create an ever-evolving loop of inspiration and innovation.

To everyone who has their work or words featured in the pages of this book, we are supremely grateful.

And finally, our deepest gratitude to the inspirational power of pattern itself. In all your infinitely inspiring manifestations from the past, present and beyond, you continue to fill us with hope and wonder at a time when the world needs it most.

ABOUT PATTERNITY

Established in 2009 by 'cult pattern pioneers' art director Anna Murray and surface designer Grace Winteringham, PATTERNITY was born from a drive to give pattern a powerful and positive voice.

Starting out as the world's only dedicated digital pattern archive, PATTERNITY quickly became an essential source of inspiration for design companies and brands around the globe. Today PATTERNITY is an international brand in its own right with a community of over 1.5 million.

With an unrivalled position as the go-to authority on pattern exploration and innovation, PATTERNITY has designed product ranges that continue to sell in major museums and select retailers internationally, branched into specialist pattern research, design and consultancy, and produced hands-on educational events for both individuals and iconic organisations. This range of diverse projects and services is connected by PATTERNITY's unique insight into the power of pattern to positively change the world around us.

PATTERNITY's award-winning approach continues to unite a wide range of individuals, specialists and institutions. From fashion and interiors to art, architecture, technology, science, psychology and nature, the PATTERNITY client and collaborator list includes: Airbnb, Apple, The Barbican, The BBC, Bompas & Parr, Celine, Clarks Originals, The Environmental Justice Foundation, Getty Images, Google, Granta, Levi's, Nike, The School of Life, Selfridges and The V&A.

True to its founding values, the PATTERNITY image archive and editorial offering at PATTERNITY.ORG remains a go-to destination for pattern seekers across the globe.

PATTERNITY's influential and democratic philosophy has attracted a large online community of pattern enthusiasts from Beijing to Boston and was cited by *The Telegraph* as one of the world's 'Top 10 Most Influential Style Blogs' and Voted 6th in *Wallpaper** Magazine's '20 Best Things on the Web'. In addition to notable industry awards and press features – in *Vogue*, *The New York Times*, *The Independent*, *The Times*, *The Telegraph*, *i-D*, *Elle* and *The Guardian* – PATTERNITY continues to establish its place as the name synonymous with pattern and progress today.

WWW.PATTERNITY.ORG